D1403057

MASKS AND MARIONETTES

THE MACMILLAN COMPANY
NEW YORK · BOSTON · CHICAGO · DALLAS
ATLANTA · SAN FRANCISCO

MACMILLAN & CO., LIMITED
LONDON · BOMBAY · CALCUTTA
MELBOURNE

THE MACMILLAN COMPANY
OF CANADA, LIMITED
TORONTO

JOSEPH SPENCER KENNARD
DOCTOR OF THE SORBONNE, PARIS

MASKS
AND
MARIONETTES

BY

JOSEPH SPENCER KENNARD

NEW YORK

THE MACMILLAN COMPANY

1935

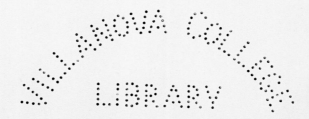

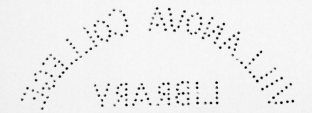

TO

𝕴. 𝕭. 𝕶.

In Memoriam

CONTENTS

MASKS

vii

CONTENTS

ILLUSTRATIONS

BELLO[...]
[...]RAINVTIVS FARN[...]SIV[...]
AVGVSTA MA[...]IF[...]

PROSCENIUM, ARCH AND C[...]

EATRVM
TI DVX. IV. CASTRI V.
MDCXVIII

NESE THEATRE, PARMA, 1618

MASKS

Chapter I

Origin of the Commedia dell'Arte

THE *Commedia dell'Arte* is Art and it is Psychology. It is a theatre of all people, of all arts, of all moments when life wings up out of drab reality. It is a theatre of music and dance; of song, colour and light; of plays on wagon stages; of festivals in streets, in courts, in great squares; on rivers; at weddings and funerals and coronations; of actors with and without masks; sometimes in extraordinary costumes.

Many of these actors are unknown to fame; many more are immortal. Paintings, etchings and engravings have made their faces familiar—diverting, ludicrous, facetious; sometimes grimly, often grotesquely, the *Commedia dell'Arte* portrays incongruous humanity.

The first comic actor may have stood on a rock, a tree stump or by evening fire in front of his hut. He postured, grimaced, gesticulated, told a funny story, cracked a joke, sang a song, burlesqued a boon companion. The *Commedia dell'Arte* developed through the ages and includes such plays as Goldoni's, which will live forever; but always the *Commedia dell'Arte* depicts human frailties, parodies human foibles.

Eight hundred years before Christ a drivelling, pot-bellied drunkard was represented on the Grecian stage. Centuries later Icarian jesters with trestles and carts gave performances in Grecian cities. Athenian and Spartan charlatans drolled and clowned to attract an audience and sell their medicines.

3

Roman theatrical art is derived from the Etruscan. Maccus, Bucco, Pappus and Casnar, speaking in Oscan, Greek and Latin, improvised plays called *Atellanæ*. The Roman *Mimi* were farceurs who declaimed; the *Pantomimi* gestured, danced and mimicked—sometimes to the accompaniment of music. The *Sanniones* resembled modern circus clowns. In their long dresses, shaven heads, painted faces and parti-coloured coats the *Planipedes* suggest the modern harlequin. The obscene *Ithyphalli* and *Phallophori* have disappeared. Oscans from the town of Atella near Naples performed *Atellanæ Fabulæ* or *Ludi Osci;* and *Maccus,* like the modern *Pulcinella,* from under his mask amused Romans with wit and satire. *Pulcinella's* ancestral statues in bronze have been found in Herculaneum; and on the walls of Pompeii his portraits are seen, beak-nose and all.

An enormous helmet made at first of tree bark and later of leather covered the head of the actor. During the reign of the Emperor Adrian, Alulu-gelle wrote: "The whole head and face of the actor was enclosed within the mask in such a manner that the voice could escape through only one part which rendered the voice stronger and more distinct." Because of this holding and reverberating of the voice the Latins called these masks *personæ*. They were comic, tragic or—when representing satyrs or Cyclopes—were ugly and of great size. In the Terence comedies the masks represented the characters but concealed the actor's personality. Since female parts were always acted by men the mask sometimes represented a woman's headdress and ornaments.

In Greek and Roman theatres of the fourth and fifth centuries, deceived husbands, philosophers and physicians were ridiculed. This type of play passed directly to the Italian theatre. In 560 A.D. Cassiodorus writes that the pantomime

ITALIAN *COMMEDIA DELL'ARTE*
OR IMPROMPTU COMEDY

was extremely popular among the Romans; and we know that the Emperor Augustus frequented the performances of the pantomimist Bathyllus. In time of famine the Emperor Constantius expelled the philosophers from Rome but allowed three thousand dancers and as many pantomimists to remain. Seneca relates that twenty thousand gold crowns were given to a favourite female dancer on her marriage.

Lucian composed a treatise on pantomimes. According to Macrobius, when Hylas danced a Hymn ending with the words "the great Agamemnon," he drew himself erect to express the meaning; but pantomimist Pylades said "you make him tall but not great." Then Pylades danced the same Hymn and when he came to this passage he assumed the posture of deep meditation. Apuleius describes a performance where the whole story of the "Judgment of Paris" was told by dance and gesture. Appianus Alexandrinus mentions a pantomime play describing the destruction of Crassus and his army by the Parthians. Suetonius relates that Nero, being ill, vowed that when well he would dance the story of Turnus as told in the Æneid.

Ferrarius asserts that as late as 1719 vestiges of these Roman pantomimes still existed in Italy, and that the *Mattaccini* of Lombardy gave performances which were survivals of the old pantomimic dances of the *Luperci*. Clothed in a tight-fitting dress and wearing masks of old men they ran through the streets, dancing, beating people with *"ecourgees,"* like the ancient *Luperci*. They ran before fast-driven carriages, climbed walls, entered windows and engaged in mock combat; one falling and pretending to be dead, his dancing partner would lift him up and carry him away. He relates how a company of masked and dancing *Mattaccini* visited a young man on his wedding day while surrounded by his friends. When one of the dancers whispered in the bridegroom's ear he arose and mixed in the masquerade, engaged in a feigned combat with one of the other dancers and according to the custom of this dance dropped down as if dead. The others carried him into a neighbouring chamber swaying to the accompaniment of lugubrious music, as if attending a funeral. After the dancers had left, the guests found the bridegroom on the floor, strangled by his rival who had been one of the dancers.

Callot engraved that famous series of buffoons, mimes and masks of the ancient comedy known as *Balli di Sfessania*. In ancient times the Sfessania in Piedmont invented a popular verse characterized by improvised pleasantries, postures and scenes resembling the *Atellanæ*. In Rome these actors were called *Mimi Septentrionis*, buffoons of the north. Naked or clad only with a waist scarf they accompanied themselves with castanets. Callot's types were mostly real actors among whom is *"Covilelo,"* renowned for his comical faces and manner of speaking. Salvatore Rossa says that *Covilelo* was one of the seven masks of the ancient *Commedia dell'Arte;* that he originated in Calabria and had the accent and costume of his country. He resembles the *"trasone"* of Terence.

The early Fathers of the Church fulminated against pagan comedies; but the Church victorious, forgetting the simplicity of early Christian worship, gave sanctuary to dramatic art and religious drama became a part of the sacred service. Crusaders from the Holy Land and Constantinople filled all Europe with tales of miracles, marvels and knightly adventures; and this fantastic material was added to the ancient Latin farces, improvisations and *lazzi*. About 1589 Niccolò Rossi wrote "Nor will I ever name as comedies these that are carried here and there by sordid and mercenary folk, introducing therein Gianni, Bergamasco, Francatrippa, Pantalone and such-like buffoons, did we not wish to resemble them to the *Mimes, Atellanæ* and *Planipedes* of the ancients." Vincenzo de Amicis noted the likeness between the Roman and *Commedia dell' Arte* characters; with their droll voices, gesticulations, somersaults, dances and *lazzi*. The "Zanni" is the Latin *Sannio*. The Doctor is *Dossennus*. Pantalone is *Pappus*. Pulcinella, dressed in white, is *Maccus* or *Bucco* or *Mimus Albus;* and bizarre multi-coloured Arlecchino is *Mimus Centunculus*. The elements of the popular Italian comedy are the oldest, most vital, most national possessions of the race; an Italian comedy of masks and improvisations which flourished before Rome rose upon the Tiber.

It has been said that to connect the *Commedia dell'Arte* with the ancient Mime would require a continuity of literary texts of the same character through the whole Middle Ages and that no such compositions exist; that Pulcinella and Arlecchino alone even remotely link the *Commedia dell'Arte* with the Latin theatre; and that to make this association probable it would be necessary to prove that in the second half of the fifteenth century Greek actors emigrated to Italy, and there presented comic plays modelled from the Turko-Byzantine type of Mime, and that these comic figures preserved their character throughout the whole Cinquecento. Lorenzo Stoppato collected many evidences tending to prove this continuity; and Ermano Reich maintains that the Italian *Commedia dell'Arte* is the natural transformation of the Byzantine Mime—which passed into Italy at the time of the great emigration after the Turks captured Constantinople, together with the remnants of the ancient Latin Mime which had feebly survived through the Middle Ages.

As in the Roman so in the Italian *Commedia dell'Arte,* dialects were spoken, masks used; and rank realism and

obscenity were equally common to the Italian masks of the sixteenth century and to the Roman masks of the fifth century
B.C. The conventional characters of Plautus and Terence reappeared. Both in Roman and in Italian plays plots were
amorous, indecent—men and women appearing naked on the
stage and unmentionable vices being boldly paraded.

Whatever may have been the origin of the Italian *Commedia dell'Arte* we know that early in the sixteenth century
improvised comedies were performed in the courts of princes,
in the palaces of lords and in academic halls, by actors each
time freshly enrolled and instructed who returned to their
ordinary occupations when the festival was over.

In 1502 Isabella Gonzaga, Marchioness of Mantua, returned to the paternal palace at Ferrara to attend the marriage of her brother the Duke with Lucrezia Borgia and was
present at a performance of Plautus' "Bacchide." Isabella
wrote her husband of the two "Moresche" dances and pantomimes interposed in the "Bacchide." One of these consisted
of ten men naked except for a scarf, their heads covered with
hair made of tin foil. In their hands they carried cornucopias
filled with varnish, with lighted tapers inside, which soon ig-
nited. A terrified maiden ran to the back of the stage; a
dragon sought to devour her but a warrior captured the beast,
and led him away bound, while the maiden arm in arm with a
youth followed him; and round about them went those naked
men tossing flames in the air. The second act was of madmen
wearing shirts and stockings and on their heads paper fools-
caps, having bladders in their hands with which they beat
each other. This was true *Commedia dell'Arte*.

In Florence, the Dramatic Art found in the "Cento No-
velle" abundance of plots, characters, caricatures, jests and
repartee. The form of this new material was always Plautinian

or Terentian, but the ancient monotony was broken. Thus, the "Calandria" * is decked with episodes borrowed from the "Decameron"; and the "Mandragola" † in its scenic art follows the Latin model. Says the poet in the prologue

> Un amante meschino,
> Un Dottor poco astuto,
> Un Frate mal vissuto,
> Un Parassito di malizia il cucco,
> Fien questo giorno il vostro badalucco.

An unhappy Lover, a Doctor who is a simpleton, a dissolute Friar, a Sycophant who is the very essence of cunning, provide your pastime for today.

As spectacular scenes grew more popular acting became a profession. Lasca published a popular carnival song referring to professional actors (1559). The *Graziana* company and also the *Compagnia della Flaminia* and that of Vincenza Armani recited at Mantua (1567). Comedy or tragedy performances had now become an "art." The *Commedia* with its many masks and dialects and improvised recitation was now called *dell'Arte*. Florentine pedants distrusted the new fashion. Varchi in his "Suocera" declared that his play was "neither wholly ancient nor wholly modern but partly modern and partly ancient" and added, "although it is in the Florentine tongue it is adapted from the Latin; adapted, I say, and not translated; unless in the same sense as the Latins translated from the Greeks." And Salviati declaimed in the prologue of the "Granchio"

> Nuova Dûnque è questa Commedia, e a tutto
> Potere di colui che I'ha fatta,
> Fatta a imitazione delle antiche;
> Di quello antiche però che gli antichi

* A play by Cardinal Bibbièna.
† A play by Machiavelli.

> Chiamavan nuove, adunque non in prosa
> Ma in versi. . . .

This comedy is new, and is to the best of the author's ability composed in imitation of the ancient comedies; of those ancient comedies, however, which the ancients themselves called "new"; that is to say, written in verse not prose.

Even in those days, however, the public knew how to make its rights respected and Il Lasca informs us

> Lionardo Salviati muor di duolo
> Perchè il suo Granchio fu tanto achernito!

And Lionardo Salviati dies of grief because his "Granchio" was so much ridiculed.

People were weary of plots contrived by crafty servants against stupid masters, the amours of vainglorious soldiers and the boastings of parasites—performances far removed from reality—and they applauded Gelli's prologue of the "Sporta." "The play being a mirror of customs in private and civic life treats only of such things as happen every day of our life. The place wherein the action moves is your Florence; and this the author has selected because it would not be possible for him to choose a place that both to you and to him should be more acceptable and because the greater number of the events that you will see have in their time taken place and perhaps still take place in Florence; and should it prove necessary, he would be able to tell you to whom and how." And welcome was given to another shoemaker actor:

> Apollo vuol che sempre un calzaiuolo
> Per lui tenga in Firenze il principato,
> E sia nel far commedie unico e solo

Apollo always wishes that a shoemaker should hold preeminence for him in Florence, and be unique in the composition of plays.

Il Lasca observed to Lotto:

> Ch'Ulisse e Turno da parte lasciando,
> Dimostra solo a questa età presente
> Ruggier, Gradasso, Marfisa ed Orlando;
> E Menandro e Terenzio ha per niente,
> Ma sol Giovan Boccaccio va imitando;
> Onde moderne fa con gran ragione
> Commedie che non hanno paragone.

Who, leaving aside Ulysses and Turnus, shows to this present age only Ruggier, Gradasso, Marfisa and Orlando; and lightly esteeming Menander and Terence, imitates Giovanni Boccaccio; thus with great good sense composing in modern form unequalled comedies.

This does not mean, however, that the *Commedia dell'Arte* did not use these same subjects, presenting them under the "maschere" which had become so popular; and, when masked as Pedrolino or Captain Spavento, the public gladly accepted the "Miles Gloriosus" and "Servo" of the Plautinian and Terentian Comedies.

And the fertile Cecchi in the "Assiuolo" presented a play which he affirmed to be "perfectly new" and "not derived from either Terence or Plautus but from a thing recently befallen in Pisa between certain young students and certain ladies." . . .

> A giudizio del popolo fiorentino
> E delle donne, che piú pesa e grava,
> Il Cecchi ha vinto e superato il Cino
> Che prima era un poeta e scaccafava

In the opinion of the Florentine people and, what is yet more important, in that of the women, Cecchi has conquered and surpassed Cino * who was rather a poet and *scaccafava*.†

---

* Cino da Pistoia, a poet of the *dolce stil nuovo*.

† *Scaccafava:* a name given to a kind of slipper.

In the prologue of his *Suppositi,* Ariosto (1474–1533) declares "the author confesses to you that in this work he has
followed Plautus and Terence since not only in the style but
also in the subject of the tales he strives with all his power to
imitate the ancient and celebrated poets. As they in their
Latin plays followed Menander and Apollodorus and the
other Greeks."

Yet Ariosto in the prologue of his first play had coura-
geously repudiated those prejudices to which now he clings.

> Nova commedia v'appresento, piena
> Di varii giochi, che nè mai latine
> Nè greche lingue recitarno in scena.
> Parmi veder che la più parte incline
> A riprenderla, subito ch'ho detto
> Nova, senza ascoltarne mezzo o fine;
> Chè tale impresa non li par suggetto
> Delli moderni ingegni, e solo stima
> Quel che li antiqui han detto esser perfetto.
> È ver che nè volgar prosa nè rima
> Ha paragon con prose antique o versi,
> Nè pari è l'eloquentia a quella prima;
> Ma gl'ingegni non son però diversi
> Da quel che fûr; ch'ancor per quell'artista
> Fansi, per cui nel tempo addietro fêrsi!

I present to you here a new comedy full of varied jests such as
never did Latin or Greek actors perform upon the stage. It seems
to me that the majority inclines to raise the objection so soon as
I have said "New," without listening to either my method or my
aim, that such an enterprise does not seem to them adapted for
modern talents and that they esteem only as perfect the work of
the ancient writers. It is true that neither Italian prose nor rhyme
is equal in value to the ancient verse nor is it so eloquent. Still,
talents are not different from what they were and are ready to
serve artists who possess them as they did formerly.

The Italian comedy of the Renaissance is an imitative form

of art patterned chiefly after Plautus and Terence, from whom plots were borrowed and sometimes whole scenes taken with scarcely any change except the substitution of Italian names and something of sixteenth century Italian atmosphere in place of the Roman. Ariosto's *Cassaria* is probably the first Italian comedy composed after the model of the Latin comedians. In his later comedies sometimes he gets away from the Romans and gives us direct transcripts of contemporary life as he saw it in Ferrara, Mantua, Rome and Venice. Ariosto's *La Lena* was played with great pomp in Ferrara in 1528 or 1529. It is the most realistic and original of Ariosto's comedies; an accurate study of contemporary low life in Ferrara.

The final and entirely refashioned *Cassaria,* written in verse in accordance with classical ideals, was presented in Ferrara in 1531 and had a tremendous success. Geraldi and other contemporary critics held it to be the best comedy of the age. The general public, however, repudiated Ariosto's "improvements" and Il Lasca wrote:

> In fino ad oggi non s'è recitate
> Commedia in versi mai che sia piaciuta;
> E la Cassaria, in versi transmutata,
> Nel recitarsi non fu conosciuta.

Till today there never was recited any play in verse which satisfied; and *Cassaria* translated into verse was not recognized when recited.

When the Duke of Mantua wished to celebrate the second descent into Italy of Charles V he asked Ariosto for a play, and four were sent. All were returned with a letter saying that "although the plots of all may be fine and excellently written, none the less it does not please me to have them acted in verse; if you have the last two written in prose, and also the

Cassaria (which you have now patched and changed into verse), I shall be pleased for you to make me a copy and will add this new obligation to the one I am already under to you for having sent the present versions which are truly more artistic and learned but do not seem so successful as when performed in prose." Mortified Ariosto replied to the duke "It seemed to me that they were better thus than in prose; but opinions differ."

It is most interesting and significant that Don Ercole invited Ruzzante and his company to Ferrara in 1529, and that they danced and sang the evening after the performance of Ariosto's *Cassaria* and that Ariosto, the greatest of the Renaissance writers of classic comedy should have directed the dramatic performances in Ferrara of the carnival of 1532, including a comedy after the type of the *Commedia dell'Arte* given by Ruzzante and his company.

Meantime, whilst this heated dispute was going on between the Florentine "Literati" there appeared on the scene a company of actors and the people ran in crowds to the "Stanza" (for so their little theatre was called), abandoning Cecchi and Lotto and Cino and Buonanni, who looked very blank when these strolling players were allowed to inaugurate the new "Salone della Commedia."

Il Lasca rubs his hands and laughs behind their backs.

> Tutti i comici nostri florentini
> Son per questa cagione addolorati;
> Prima il Buonanni e la casa de' Cini
> Si favoriti e tanto adoperati;
> E Lotto e il Cecchi alfin, piccin piccini,
> Con tutti gli altri dotti, son restati,
> Parendo questa sorta loro arcigna,
> E il Lasca chiude l'occhiolino a ghigna.
> Pensando il primo ognuno essere richiesto,

La sua commedia aveva apparecchiato:
Chi l'aveva mostra a quello e chi a questo,
Sperando d'ora in ora essere chiamata;
Ma il popol pol weggendo manifesto
L'onor dei Zanni in fino al cielo alzato,
Senza piú altro intendere o sapere,
Altre commedie non vuol piú vedere.
Si che chi n'ha cemposte ne dia loro,
Pregando che le vogliono accettare;
Poi che ne fanno tanto buon lavoro,
Ch'ogni cosuzza una gran cosa pare.
La voce, gli atti e i gesti di costoro
Si graziosi fan maravigliare
La gente alfin fuor d'ogni umana guisa,
E quasi quasi crepar delle risa.
Non credo mai che gl'istron passati,
Volete in Rome o volate in Atene,
Si capricciosi giuochi e si garbati
Rappresentasser nell'antiche scene.
Sei quei fur buon, questi son vantaggiati,
Questi fan meglio se quei fecer bene;
Onde assai plú di lor fieno I Gelosi
Nei secoli avvenir sempre famosi.

All our Florentine playwrights are in distress on this account. Buonanni and the family of Cini, so popular and so successful; then Lotto and Cecchi and other learned men have lost courage; this being a bitter pill for them; while Il Lasca winks and grins. Each expecting to be the first called for had prepared his play; some had shown their work to this one, others to that one, hoping from hour to hour to be summoned; but the people seeing the glory of the "Zanni" rise to the very skies, without wanting to hear or know anything further refuse to see any other plays. So let anyone who has composed one give it to these actors begging them to accept it; and they will act it so well that the smallest trifle will appear a fine piece of work. The voices, actions and gestures of these players are so charming that they amaze the people and make them almost split their sides with laughter. I do not believe that any actors of the past, whether in Rome or in Athens, ever performed so charmingly and gracefully on the ancient stage. If those were good, these do better what the others did well; hence, even more than they shall the Gelosi be honoured in future centuries.

The Company of "I Gelosi" had arrived in Florence. It was the most famous of all the Companies which during two centuries performed the *Commedia dell'Arte* in Italy and abroad. It had as its ensign a two-faced Janus with the motto which gave rise to its name:

"Virtu, fama ed onor ne fer Gelosi."

They were jealous for the attainment of virtue, fame and honour.

Francesco Andreini, for many years leader of the *Gelosi*, exclaims in one of his dialogues, "Trappola *mio,* no longer are such Companies to be found; and this may be confidently asserted respecting those that have but three or four good actors, the others being of little use and not equal to the chief actors of that famous Company where every rôle was remarkable. So fine was it in fact that in the dramatic art it set a standard beyond which no company of actors could go, and set an example for future actors as to how best to compose and interpret comedies and the other performances such as are generally seen upon the stage."

> Facendo il Bergamasco e'l Veneziano,
> N'andiamo in ogni parte,
> E'l recitar commedie è la nostr'arte. . . .
> Questi vostri dappochi commediai
> Certe lor filastroccole vi fanno,
> Lunghe e piene di guai,
> Che rider poco e manco piacer dànno;
> Tanto che per l'affanno,
> Non solamente agli uomini e alle donne,
> Ma verrebbero a noia alle colonne.

Acting the Bergamask and the Venetian we roam the whole world over, and the performing of comedies is our trade. These silly comedians of yours act for you certain foolish plays of theirs which, long and tedious, give little amusement and less pleasure; so tiresome are they in fact that they bore not only men and women but even the pillars.

And he invited the citizens to come

> . . . alla Stanza ad udir Zanni,
> La Nespola, il Magnifico e'l Graziano,
> E Francatrippa che vale un tesoro,
> E gli altri dicitor di mano in mano,
> Che tutti fanno bene gli atti loro!

To the Stanza to hear Zanni, La Nespola, il Magnifico and Graziano, and Francatrippa who is a treasure in himself, and the other actors, one after another, who all perform their parts well.

Flaminio Scala, "Flavio," was still the same "Magnifico Pantalone" who had aroused the admiration of Henry III. Graziano the Bolognese pedant was Ludovico de' Bianchi, the most famous interpreter of that type since the time when he acted with Ganassa a "Lus Burchiello Gratia." Il Lasca describes the way in which he took off his cap:

> Che gentilmente la piglia con mano,
> Poi la scuote e dimena con gran fretta;
> E quanto l'usa più di dimenare
> Più vuol amico o signore onorare.

Which he gracefully takes with his hand; then shakes it and twists it in great haste, and the more he wishes to honour friend or signor the more he twists it round.

Chapter II

Famous Players and Famous Companies

ANGELO BEOLCO, surnamed Ruzzante (the joker), born at
Padua in 1502, was an early and famous actor in the *Commedia
dell'Arte*. Bernardino Scardeon's "Antiquities of
Padua" (1560) relates that "Angelo Beolco, known under the
name of Ruzzante, was to Padua what Plautus had been to
Rome as an author and Roscius as an actor. He even surpassed
them; and there is no ancient comedy comparable to those
which Ruzzante played throughout Italy. When he was on
the stage the public had neither eyes nor ears for any of the
other actors." *

Ruzzante lived in the midst of the Italian wars of Francis I
and of Charles V. Rome was assaulted, Florence ravaged by
pest and Ruzzante's Padua desolated by famine. His comedies
fulminate against both the Spanish and the German. Amidst
his most amusing improvisations there are terrible situations,
seething passion. Ruzzante inspired the Italian comedy revival and its use of popular dialects. His characters speak
Paduan, Bergamask, Bolognese, Venetian, Tuscan, Latin,
Italianized Spanish and modern Greek.

Ruzzante filled the principal rôle in his own plays, sometimes wearing an archaic or fantastic costume. When he ap-

---

* In 1617 at Vicenzo, Domenico Amadio printed "The Works of the most celebrated Signor Angelo Beolco, a noble Paduan surnamed Ruzzante. They are greatly
loved and appreciated throughout the entire world for their sentiment, esprit,
finesse and the learning with which they are full."

pears on the stage he says: "Let us amuse ourselves. You will never guess my name and I won't ask you to try. I am a mad spirit or goblin. I come from the other world and one of those spirits called Actius or Plautus orders me to tell you that a comedy will be played this evening. It is not composed in Latin, in verse or in beautiful language, nor would those ancient actors compose their comedies today in a different manner from that which you shall hear."

Padua is the scene of Ruzzante's play *Moschetta;* peasants are the principal characters. Ruzzante would test his wife's fidelity. Angry Bettina flies to a soldier's house. Ruzzante's attempts to win her back make excellent comedy. In the *Fiorina* comedy Ruzzante and Merchioro contend for Fiore's favours. Ruzzante's jealous rival beats him but he carries off the prize. This short swift comedy is virile, simple and sober art. Ruzzante appeals to the young contadina. "But what sweetness, what joy to me to die at thy dear hands, my beautiful Fiore; for thou art dearer to me than my oxen." How spontaneous and ingenuous the comparison! How characteristic of the Italian peasant!

In the *Dialoghi in lingua rustica* entitled *Parlamento de Ruzzante che era vegnu de campo* (Speech of Ruzzante on coming from the field), Ruzzante is the typical braggart poltroon; repulsed by Gnua, beaten by her "bravo" lover, he becomes valiant when the "bravo" departs. *Belora* is a monologue describing a poor peasant's emotions when robbed of his wife. He will murder the seducer but renounces his intention. He would beat and insult, yet he is not brave; his honour is not sensitive. But he loves his faithless wife, will have her and will beat her. It is a tremendous part, fraught with laughter, tears and terror.

Ruzzante's Fiorina or Fiorinetta is a sixteenth century

replica of the Philenie of Demophile and of Plautus. But there is a difference. Plautus' Philenie is a loving courtesan, who shares her favours with both father and son; after having been caressed by two slaves. Unlike Philenie, Fiorinetta loves Flavio with her whole soul.

FIORINETTA: What do you wish from me, mother?

CELEGA: To my great distress you have again permitted Flavio to enter the house by the garden gate. I have not said anything to you about his presence. . . . Stupid child, do you not realize your misfortune? If you love those who give you nothing, all the others will keep their hands closed. Our future depends upon competition. A hundred times I have told you, if anyone makes you a present show it to the others and they will give you something more valuable. Be charming to everyone and pretend that you love them all.

FIORINETTA: Do you wish me to love everybody as I love Flavio?

CELEGA: I don't tell you to love anybody but to make believe that you love them.

FIORINETTA: My mother, that would be for me a life of great suffering. I can do nothing contrary to the feelings which I have in my heart. I would rather marry; and I wish for a happier existence than that which you propose for me.

Fiorinetta has never been a courtesan. She has none of the sentiments or attractions of one. Better die than belong to anyone except her dear Flavio. When Flavio's mother Rospina consents to this marriage she realizes this. She would never have received Philenie, the courtesan of the antique drama. This is a better play than Plautus at his best. Ruzzante, the Renaissance buffoon, possessed something akin to Shakespeare and Molière. He played his comedies impromptu before he wrote them, and in many scenes the improvisation is left to the actors. Andrea Calmo (1540), Venetian contemporary of Beolco (Ruzzante), was both actor and playwright; his *Saltuzza, Rodiana* and *Travaglia* resemble classic comedies. His other plays are true *Commedia dell'Arte,* intermingling dialects, literary Italian and Italo-German jargon. His "Letters" are a shower of jokes, satire and jest; a river of words rippling with laughter.

Gigio Artemio Giancarli of Rovigo was both author and actor. In his *Capriria* and *Zingana* he used many dialects. The title "Capriria" is derived from certain she-goats which the peasant Spadan carries to his old master. Afrone's two children, brother Lionello and sister Dorotea meet after a long separation but fail to recognize one another. Both Afrone and Lionello love Dorotea; Afrone is tricked and cheated by his servant Brusca but Lionello is faithfully served by Orteca, inexhaustible deviser of cunning plans. Lively, witty, amusing, this play has a marked classical character.

The *Zingana* comedy transforms the old *motifs* and adds new ones drawn from life. It is an excellent Cinquecento popular drama. An old married couple Alcario and Barbarina love Stella and Cassandro, but finally recover from their senile desires. The *Zingana* contains many comic scenes; is rich in jests and gay conceits and unforeseen happenings. In Ruzzante's, Calmo's and Giancarli's plays the professional comedians preferred improvisation to memorized repetition and one actor played many parts. This improvisation and the fixed types that these artists probably borrowed from plebeian farce finally became essential characteristics of a special kind of dramatization which formed the connecting link between the learned and the popular theatre, the natural passage from the literary comedy of classic type to the *Commedia dell'Arte.* Thus in the second half of the sixteenth century rose the "Art Comedy" whose characteristic was improvisation and masks.

In 1570 an Italian company of comedy actors came to Paris and on their little stage presented farces and comedies in

French, Italian and Spanish. In 1571 the first "principal" company of *"Comici d'arte"* arrived in Paris to celebrate the' entry of King Charles IX with his bride. Next year they en- livened the nuptials of the King of Navarre with the sister of the French King. This Gelosi Company was led by a Berga- mese stage-named "Ganassa," who perhaps invented the rôle of Arlequino, the second Zanni. By direction of the Duke of Mantova, Ganassa merged his company with that directed by "Pantalone"; hence Brantôme referred to their plays as "celles de Zanni et Pantalone" and a certain Monsieur Vauquelin de la Fresnaye immortalized in his verse

> Ou le bon Pantalon, ou Zany dont Ganasse
> Nous a represente la façon et la grace

Either the good Pantalone or Zany whose manners and grace Ganassa has represented for us.

In October 1571 the Gelosi Company was still at Paris; in 1572 at Genoa; but Ganassa with part of his company was playing in Spain. The company "des comediantes Italianos, cuya cabeza y autor era Alberto Ganassa," received a warm welcome there. It performed "comedias Italianas, mímicas" for "la mayor parte y bufonescas de asuntos triviales y popu- lares," in which figured "las personas de Arlequín, del Panta- lón, del Dotore, etc."; and we are told that even if Ganassa was not "perfectly understood" there he made the assembly laugh and obtained much money, and that from him the Spaniards learned to make plays similar to his. Those mem- bers of the Gelosi Company who had not followed Ganassa into Spain played in Venice during the carnival of 1574 and later in Milan during the festivals honouring Don Giovanni of Austria, hero of Lepanto. When Catherine de' Medici's son Henry King of Poland, passed through Venice, he requested

FRANCESCO ANDREINI

a performance by the Gelosi Company, and especially wished to see the famous prima donna. In 1574 the Confidenti and Gelosi united as the Comici Uniti. Later they separated and the Gelosi Company was re-formed under Flaminio Scala and again visited Paris in 1577.

In 1560 *Sofonisba,* translated by Saint-Gelais, was performed by the French King's daughters and by other ladies and young girls. The Queen, considering that this play "had brought evil to the affairs of the kingdom," banished all tragedies; though "ouy bien des comédies et tragicomédies, et mesmes celles de Zanni et Pantalone, y prenant grand plaisir, et y rioit son saoul comme une autre car elle rioit volontiers." King Henry having adjusted his affairs of state remembered his gay Venetian days and wrote to the French Ambassador at Venice

Now that peace is made in my kingdom I wish to have here the "Magnifique" . . . the one who came to me at Venice on my return from Poland with all the actors of the company of the Gelosi. I beg you to seek out the said "Magnifique" and tell him to come to me according to the letter I write him and which you will deliver to him. You will also furnish him with the money necessary for his journey, letting me know what you have given him. I will order those who attend to my finances that it be returned to you soon.   Henry.

Giulio Pasquati was in truth a "Magnifico." On January 25, 1577, Pasquati and the Gelosi Company were at Blois where King Henry had convoked the States-General, and performed before the King and his court. They arrived a little late because on the way they had been captured by the Huguenots, who obtained from the King a considerable ransom.

Francesco Andreini, born at Pistoia about 1548, was captured by the Turks but after eight years escaped from slavery. Welcomed into Scala's company, he became famous as Capitano Spavento dell' Vall' Inferno. At Milan he played the part of a Sicilian Doctor "very comic" and that of "the wizard Falsirona, who spoke French, Spanish, Slav, Greek, Turkish"; then he "marvellously acted the part of the shepherd Corinto playing many different wind instruments and singing rural verses in imitation of Sannazaro."

The Gelosi Company played before King Henry III in 1577 and afterwards at the Hôtel de Bourbon. They attracted an audience "larger than that of Paris' four most popular preachers"; grumpy judges complained that such was "the corruption of the times that farce-players, buffoons and *mignons,* all found favour with the king." Towards the end of 1602 Marie de Médicis invited the Gelosi to again visit the French Court. For nearly thirty years Flaminio Scala (Flavio), director of the Gelosi Company, was applauded in France and Italy. He first collected and printed the *scenari* of the improvised comedies. These scenarios merely explain the necessary action. This was the Gelosi Company which vexed Florentine playwrights in 1578. We have seen how Il Lasca composed a derisive poster announcing their arrival in Florence.

In 1578 Flaminio Scala engaged in the Gelosi Company a sixteen-year-old Paduan girl named Isabella, beautiful, talented and virtuous. The actor Francesco Andreini loved her at first sight and married her. Next year Isabella bore a son G. B. Andreini, afterwards famous as "Lelio." Isabella was the soul, the honour and the chief support of the Gelosi Company, praised by Tasso, Ciabrera, Marino, by cardinals, princes and kings; her crowned portrait was placed between those of

ISABELLA ANDREINI

Petrarch and Tasso in a festa given her in Rome by Cardinal Aldo Brandeni.*

Isabella left Paris and was on her way to Italy when an accident obliged her to stop in the city of Lyons, and there she died on July 10, 1604. To her funeral aldermen sent the city flags with their mace bearers; and the merchant's corporation followed the hearse with torches. A medal was struck bearing on one side her portrait and name with the letters "G.C." (Comedian of the Gelosi Company) and on the reverse the emblem of Fame and the words *"Æterna fama."* With her died the Gelosi Company.

Francesco Andreini's Capitano Spavento thus answers his servant Trappola, who has asked about the famous Gratiano of the Gelosi Company:

I have met him; and with him I have met Pasquali of Padua, the Pantalone; Simone of Bologna, the Zanne; Gabrielle of Bologna who was Francatrippa; Gratio of Padua, the "Lover"; dame Isabella Andreini of Padua who was the *prima donna* lover; and a certain Francesco Andreini, husband of the said dame Isabella. This Andreini played the part of a haughty and boastful Captain who, I well remember from my name, gave himself out as 'Capitano Spavento dell' Vall' Inferno.' "

Francesco Andreini's son Giambattista (Giovanni-Battista)

* Admired by the Court and the City, and especially by Marie de Médicis and Henry IV, her popularity in France was enormous. Of her a French poet wrote

Je ne crois point qu'Isabelle
Soit une femme mortelle;
C'est plutôt quelqu'un des dieux
Qui s'est déguisé en femme
Afin de nous ravir l'âme
Par l'oreille et par les yeux.

Thomas Garzoni in his *Piazza Universale* wrote: "The gracious Isabella Andreini, most brilliant ornament of the theatre, equally praiseworthy for her beauty and for her virtue, has rendered illustrious the profession of comedian. So long as the world endures and to the end of the centuries, the name of the celebrated Isabella Andreini will be venerated."

was known on the stage as "Lelio." He directed the Fedeli Company, largely composed of former Gelosi actors. United with the Accesi they performed in Milan in 1606 but soon separated. In 1601 Andreini married the youthful Virginia Ramponi, famous as "Florinda" as witness these lines:

> Vive la madre tua ne la tua sposa
> Chè de lo suo divin dandole parte,
> In Virginia respira e in lei si cole.

Your mother lives in your wife to whom she gives something of her own divinity. In Virginia she breathes again and is worshipped once more.

He composed for her his first play, under the name of *Florinda*. When the nuptials of Prince Francesco with Margherita of Savoy were being celebrated in Mantua (1608) the artist engaged to sing Arianna in Rinuccini's opera died of small-pox. Florinda memorized the part in six days and delighted her audience.

In the *Adone* (VII. 68) Marino, speaking of the performance, writes

> E in tal guisa Florinda udisti, o Manto,
> Là nei teatri de' tuoi regi tetti,
> D'Arianna spiegar gli aspri martiri,
> E trar da mille cor mille sospiri.

And you heard Florinda, O Mantuan, in the theatre of your palace, interpreting the bitter sufferings of Arianna, drawing from a thousand hearts a thousand sighs.

Florinda was the bright star of the Fedeli until she "left the stage of this world" (1627). Lelio's second wife (1628) the actress Virginia Rotari ("Lidia") had been his mistress for many years. Giambattista Andreini directed the Fedeli Com-

GIOVAN BATTISTA ANDREINI

pany until 1652. He composed many poems, comedies, sonnets and dialogues.

The *Commedia dell'Arte* was not a monopoly of the Andreinis. There were the Riccobonis and Fiorello, Domenico Biancolelli, Tommaso Visentino ("Tommasino"), Carlo Bertinazzi ("Carlino"), Salvatore Rosa, of whom Lippi wrote

> Pittor, passa chiunque tele imbiacca,
> Tratta d'ogni scienza *ut ex professo,*
> E in palco fa sì ben Coviel Patacca,
> Che, sempre ch'ei si muove o ch'ei favella,
> Fa proprio sgangherarti le mascella.

A painter who, no matter who may pass by, daubs at his canvases, treats of every science *ut ex professo* and on the stage acts so well the part of Coviel Patacca that whenever he moves or speaks he makes you split your very sides.

Such women as Flaminia Riccoboni and Aurelia Bianchi and that Maria Malloni ("Celia") of whom Marino wrote

> Celia s'appella, e ben del Ciel nel volto
> Porta la luce e la beltà Celeste;
> Ed oltre ancor, chè come il Cielo è bella
> E ha l'armonia del Ciel nella favella.

Celia, she is called; and truly she bears in her face something of Celestial light and beauty; besides which she is fair as the celestial region and has its music on her lips.

Another woman of the sixteenth century—a poet, musician, singer, sculptress, comedian—Vincenza Armani was born at Venice. In her honour "guns were fired" when she entered a city; jousts and tournaments were held in her name. She acted in Comedy, Pastorals and Tragedy, correctly, observing the rules of each. Here is some of her poetry:

E con le belle braccia
Mi cinge il collo e tace,
E il cor con l'alma allaccia,
Che di desio si sface,
Ond'io di piacer pieno
Le bacio il petto e il seno.
Dalla sua bocca bella
Poi colgo il cibo grato,
Io muto e tacit' ella,
Liet'ella ed io beato,
Portiam l'alte faville
Coi baci a mille a mille.
Quel che succede poi
Amor solo il può dire,
Perch'ebri ambidue noi
Nel colmo del gioire
Perdiam nei gaudi immensi
L'alma, gli spiriti e i sensi.

When her fair arms entwine
About my neck in silent joy
My heart and soul combine
In sweetest bliss without alloy;
With passion filled and rapture blest,
I kiss and kiss her heart and breast.
Of perfect love the pleasant fruit
From her sweet lips I gladly kiss.
Silent she and I quite mute
Happy she and I in bliss,
The sparks of love ascend on high
From kisses that unnumbered ply.
What happens then you well may guess
The God of Love alone can know.
Intoxication both confess—
Along the brink of joy we go
Then plunge into that gulf immense
Where lost is spirit, soul and sense.

Rosa Benozzi, celebrated under the name of "Sylvia," came to Paris with a company called by the Regent in 1716. For forty-two years she played the rôle of the woman lover with vivacity, delicacy and charm and up to the day of her death she enjoyed public favour. In different plays and those by different authors the rôle of "Sylvia" was variously treated. Sometimes she is mistress and soubrette; in other pieces she is simply soubrette and sometimes simple peasant or innocent shepherdess.

Eleanor Virginia Baletti ("Flaminia") was born in Ferrara in 1686. Her parents gave her a superior education and she became an excellent actress and a very cultivated woman, speaking several languages fluently. From her earliest years she was considered one of the best actresses in Italy. Louis Riccoboni ("Lelio"), director of a dramatic company, married her and brought her to Paris in 1716 hoping that she would assist him in a reformation of the Italian theatre. He was not successful. The French public preferred Harlequin and Scaramouche with their masks to the finest productions of the Italian classic theatre; so Flaminia and Riccoboni retired in 1732.

Between 1610 and 1612 the Fedeli Company played chiefly in Northern Italy. In 1613 the Queen Regent Marie de Médicis called them to Paris, and they acted at the Louvre and Hôtel de Bourgogne, and also before the Fontainebleau Court and at Saint-Germain. The Fedeli again visited France in 1621, 1622 and 1623. They acted at Prague and in Vienna at the Court of Ferdinand II from 1627 to 1628. In 1652 Eularia Coris, young and charming comedian in the Fedeli Company, contributed to the success of a dramatic piece entitled *la Maddalena Lasciva e Penitente*. Besides Magdalen, Martha and Lazarus the principal actors are the Archangel Michael and other angels, Divine Grace, three lovers of Magdalen, her page, butler, cook, two dwarfs and three old women of bad reputation. The first three acts consist of love scenes and festivals. Sensual Magdalen scorns sister Martha's reproof but in the third act she renounces pleasure, dons haircloth, sees visions and rises to Heaven borne on the arms of fifteen cherubims and followed by the Archangel Michael and Divine Grace.

In 1613 Andreini composed a "Sacra Rappresentazione" in five acts in verse, which was called *Adamo*. Among the characters are Adam and Eve, the Eternal Father, the Archangel Michael, Satan, Lucifer, infernal spirits, the Seven Mortal Sins, Seraphims, Angels, Death, Famine, the Body and the Serpent. It is a résumé of a fifteenth century mystery. This work is, possibly, the origin of Milton's *Paradise Lost*. "Il y a souvent," says Voltaire, "dans les choses où tout paraît ridicule ou vulgaire un coin de grandeur qui ne se fait apercevoir qu'aux hommes de génie" and Milton "découvrit à travers l'absurdité de l'ouvrage, une sublimité cachée du sujet." Although his plays contain many lewd passages Andreini afterward retired to a monastery to meditate and write on religious subjects.

Between 1574 and 1581 the Confidenti were acting in Northern Italy and in Mantua gave performances to celebrate the marriage of Vincenzo Gonzaga with Margherita Farnese. In 1582 or 1583 they divided, some of them joining the Uniti Company. Next year the Confidenti after acting in Turin and Milan went to France; in 1587 they were in Spain and between 1615 and 1620 they acted in various Italian cities. In 1639 while in Milan they were "called by the majesty of the King of France to come there and act for the entertainment of his Majesty and of the Queen." Meanwhile, the Uniti Company flourished under the protection of the lords of Mantua, Duke Guglielmo and his son Vincenzo, who loved the theatre. In 1583 they united with the Confidenti Company and called themselves the Uniti Confidenti." *

In 1600 the company of Accesi left Mantua for France at the request of Henry IV; they were warmly recommended by Vincenzo Gonzaga to the Dukes d'Aiguillon and de Nevers and were entertained at Turin by Carlo Emanuele of Savoy. They played a great part in the festivities in honour of the marriage of Henry with Marie de Médicis celebrated in Lyons in December 1600; and in January 1601 followed the Court to Paris where they remained till October. Recrossing the Alps, they visited Rome and Turin and in 1606 together with the company of the Fedeli, they acted in Milan. Arriving in Paris in 1608 they first performed before the King and Court and then at the Hôtel de Bourgogne.† The Accesi afterward acted in various Italian cities until their final performance in Florence in 1623. The Desiosi called also "of Diana" (after their

* The real artistic rival of Signora Vittoria of the Confidenti was Isabella of the Gelosi. In May 1589 for the marriage of Ferdinand de' Medici with Cristina of Lorraine the two rival artists met in Florence; on the 6th of May Vittoria acted in her most famous play *La Zingana* and on the 13th Isabella gave an astonishing performance in a piece of her own invention *La Pazzia*. After this the two rivals parted, each going her own way. The Uniti were in Florence and Mantua in 1592; then they went to Genoa and Milan and again in 1604 acted in Florence. For the year 1614 in the Uniti Company we have the following list of actors among others with the name, surname, native town and rôle: Jacomo Braga of Ferrara (Pantalone), Domenico de' Negri of Ferrara (Curzio), Silvio Fiorillo of Naples (Captain Mattamoros), Giovan Battista Fiorillo his son (Scaramuzza), Andrea Fraiacomi of Bologna (Trivellino).

† Calderoni's Company went to Germany "in the service of the Elector of Bavaria, to Munich and to Brussels"; and then to Vienna "in the service of the Emperor Leopold and of Joseph King of the Romans." In 1664 Calderoni wrote "The other evening 'Li tre finti turchi' was given, the new second Zanni acting, and it went so well that everyone left before it was finished, saying that if we had nothing better to offer they would pelt us with apples." On their return to Italy Calderoni's comedians acted in Naples and Leghorn. In 1697 they were in Brussels and later played in Augsburg and in Vienna. The young Roman Pietro Cotta played with this company; and having later assumed direction of his own company undertook to banish licentious words from his plays and to perform good plays such as Guarini's *Pastor fido* and Tasso's *Aminta*. His attempt failed; but Luigi Riccoboni was more fortunate as regards tragedy though he also was not successful in presenting comedies free from improprieties.

celebrated actress) acted in Pisa, Milan and Cremona and perhaps at Ferrara. In 1588, after a great dispute, license was conceded in Rome to the *Desiosi* to act comedies by day, but without women. *Senza donne* seeming to mean that boys took the place of actresses; as was the custom in Rome. The company is mentioned as having been in Genoa in May 1597 and at Verona in August 1599.

By command of the King, Luigi Riccoboni's company went to Paris and acted in the hall of the Petit Bourbon and then at the Palais Royal. In 1664 they received the official title "The King's Comedians of the Italian Troupe." In 1680 they were established at the Hôtel de Bourgogne and in 1684 their duties and rights were minutely determined. In 1697 they gave *La Fausse Prude,* a violent satire against Madame de Maintenon, and Louis XIV ordered the company disbanded and their theatre closed. Thus the Comédie Italienne was silent for nearly twenty years. But after the death of Louis XIV it was revived in 1716 when a new Italian troupe was called to Paris by the Regent Philippe d'Orléans. Antonio Vicentini called Thomassin made his first appearance in the rôle of Arlequin at the theatre of the Palais Royal in *Inganno fortunato.*

During these many years in Paris, the Italian Comedy fell so completely under French influence that the actors performed plays written in French by French authors. The Italian theatre thus became a French theatre except that it retained the licentiousness, buffoonery and satire, the pantomime, drollery, canzonettes and dances, in fact all the spirit of Italian impromptu comedy.

Born in Naples the famous "Tabarino" ("Tabarin" in French) came to Paris in 1618. At first he associated with the charlatan Mondor who set up an open-air theatre to draw a crowd to buy his medicine. In 1622 Tabarin was at the height of his glory. His theatre in the Place Dauphiné was crowded. In 1625 Tabarin made a tour of France and in 1630 he retired to enjoy his fortune. Tabarin's Farces are important in the *Commedia dell'Arte* repertoires. Of them Saint-Victor says "The pearls are rare but there is abundance of salt. Here one sometimes finds both Molière and La Fontaine." Such is the scene of Pouquelin. The "Bonhomme" epilogue has come from a Tabarin farce as a pearl comes from the oyster. Scapin's sack in which he imprisoned Géronte originated in the *baraque* of the Pont-Neuf plays.

The Comédie Italienne was an institution in France. Soldino, the Florentine, is called "comedian in his Majesty's suite" (1572) and Massimiano Milanino is designated "chief of the Company of Italian Comedians following the King of Navarre" (1578). A decree of Châtelet (1599) prohibits the "so-called Italian Comedians of the King" to hold performances elsewhere than in the Hôtel de Bourgogne. The Italian Comedy was definitely established in Paris in 1660 and continued until the nineteenth century, competing with the Comédie Française, the Foire and the Opéra Comique. In 1762 it absorbed the latter and took possession of its repertoire, acclaiming Carlo Goldoni as its director and poet. When Italian comedy was suppressed in the Hôtel de Bourgogne it went to the Sala Favart (1763). Losing its Royal subsidy in 1792 through the great Revolution it expired in 1801. The surviving Italian comedians of the Sala Favart united with a French company to form the Opéra Comique which acted at the Sala Feydeau.*

* The *Commedia dell'Arte* inspired Molière to create the French Comedy. The scenarios of the *Commedia dell'Arte* furnish the plots, scenes, types of characters from which Molière created *Tartufe, Le Malade imaginaire, George Dandin,* Trissotin, Sganarelle and Scapin.

The theatre of the Funambules was transformed into a theatre of pantomime and vaudeville, in which that great actor Deburau for fifteen years played pieces of old French farce, mixed with Italian phantasy. Deburau's pantomime was all that was left in France of the ancient Italian comedy. Deburau changed the Pierrot type, as Dominique had transformed Harlequin. Sometimes his Pierrot is good and generous, sometimes a thief; sometimes coward, sometimes brave. Almost always poor; when he had money he spent it recklessly. Always he is lazy and greedy. Deburau also transformed the physical character of his Pierrot. In Jules Janin's biography of Deburau he says:

The greatest comedian of our time was born the 31st of July, 1796. He made a revolution in our art and has created a new type. An actor without passion, without words and almost without a face, he said everything, expressed everything, mocked at everything and without speaking a single word played the comedies of Molière and gave to them real life; an inimitable genius who went hither and thither, who looked, who opened his mouth, who closed his eyes, made everyone laugh and was charming. In *Noces de Pierrot,* a farce which he played over six hundred times, we see the curtain rising slowly. Deburau appears in his white costume with a pretty girl on his arm. It is impossible to describe the enthusiasm of the audience. Deburau simply placed his hand on his heart, and a tear rolled down over his face whitened with flour.

The only Italian parts now remaining in French plays are Pierrot, Arlequin, Leandro, Cassandra and Columbine; all greatly transformed.

The *Commedia dell'Arte* exerted considerable influence upon the English comedy. In 1527 an Italian company crossed to England, led by a Mantuan, the Harlequin Drusiano Martinelli. At the court of Elizabeth the two English buffoons Tarleton and Wilton probably learned from him how to improvise on mere "scenarios" and to compose them. We still have the scenari of four comedies *dell'Arte* from the time of Elizabeth. Writers of the Elizabethan period frequently express admiration for the Italian *Commedia dell'Arte,* and reproduce the traditional comic characters in their own comedies.

Shakespeare's comedies contain many reminiscences of the *Commedia dell'Arte.* His *Comedy of Errors* is derived from the *Menechmi* through an Italian imitation; *The Taming of the Shrew* comes in part from Ariosto's *Suppositi;* and *Romeo and Juliet* recalls Luigi Groto's *Hadriana.* In *Othello* Iago calls Brabanzio "il Magnifico"; treating him as Pantalone. Captain Parolles in *All's Well That Ends Well* who carries "the whole theorick of war in the knot of his scarf and the practice in the chape of his dagger" is Capitano Spavento. The scene in which his soldiers blindfold and lead him to his own general, whom he believes to be that of the enemy and to whom he reveals the secrets of the camp and slanders his colleagues, was taken directly from an Italian scenario. In *Love's Labour's Lost* the "Spanish Captain" says to his valet:

I will hereupon confess I am in love; and as it is base for a soldier to love, so am I in love with a base wench. If drawing my sword against the humour of affection would deliver me from the reprobate thought of it I would take Desire prisoner and ransom him to any French courtier for a new devised courtesy. I think scorn to sigh; methinks I should outswear Cupid. Comfort me, boy; what great men have been in love?

The pedant Holofernes in the same comedy resembles the Italian Graziano.

Many Italian words occur in *The Taming of the Shrew* and there is even a scrap of dialogue. One friend says: "Con tutto il cuore ben trovato" and the latter replies: "Alla nostra casa ben venuto, molto honorato signor mio Petruchio." There is also a scene in which nothing of the *Commedia dell'Arte* is lacking. . . . A young man disguised as a master of grammar makes love to his lady. An old gallant is present; he too in love with this girl.

> BIANCA: Where left we last?
> LUCENTIO: Here, madam.
>   "Hac ibat Simois; hic est Sigeia tellus;
>   Hic steterat Priami regia celsa senis."
> BIANCA: Construe them.
> LUCENTIO: "Hac ibat," as I told you before, "Simois," I am Lucentio, "hic est," son unto Vincentio of Pisa, "Sigeia tellus," disguised thus to get your love; "Hic steterat," and that Lucentio that comes a-wooing, "Priami," is my man Tranio, "regia," bearing my port, "celsa senis," that we might beguile the old pantaloon. . . .
> BIANCA: Now let me see if I can construe it: "Hac ibat Simois," I know you not, "hic est Sigeia tellus," I trust you not; "Hic steterat Priami," take heed he hear us not, "regia," presume not, "celsa senis," despair not.

In *The Merry Wives of Windsor* there is the French physician who lards his discourses with phrases in his own language; and the parish priest who prattles English like a Welshman; and the silly fellow who speaks "in punta di forchetta." All these have their prototypes in improvised *Commedia*.

Every history of the *Commedia dell'Arte* must take account of Louis Riccoboni ("Lelio") who was born at Medina in 1674. Son of a celebrated actor he was both excellent actor and distinguished author, composing more than thirty plays and writing a history of the Italian theatre. According to Riccoboni there were few good actors "towards 1680." The only good company remaining being directed by Francesco Calderoni ("Silvio") and his wife Agatha ("Flaminia"). In the eighteenth century (1747) Gerolamo Medebac directed his own company in Venice, originally formed of mountebanks. Goldoni writes that this company was able within a short time "to hold its own with the oldest and most accredited companies of Italy." Antonio Sacchi's dramatic company was also active in Venice at the same time and was protected by Carlo Gozzi. In 1761 Cesare d'Arbes was one of the company, and also Teodora Bartoli Ricci who was the willing object of Carlo Gozzi's "protection," of Pietro Antonio Gratarol's love and of Sacchi's libertinism. In 1742 Sacchi (Truffaldino) the principal actor went with half his company to Russia where he remained until 1745. After 1780 Sacchi's company began to disintegrate. Sacchi when nearly eighty years of age acted in the Falcone theatre of Genoa (1786). He died on shipboard (1788) and with him died the *Commedia dell'Arte.*

Chapter III

Composition of the Dramatic Companies
Joys and Sorrows of the Players

THREE women and seven men, ten actors in all; was the usual composition of a *Commedia dell'Arte* Company. Isabella, Vittoria, Flaminia, Celia, Flavia, Silvia, Leonora, Teodora, Alvira, are maidens, shepherdesses, princesses and queens. They are maidens sometimes secretly married; or dissatisfied wives, or young widows seeking new marriage-beds. All are sentimental, athirst for love; but husbands are vigilant; and fathers are avaricious and insist on hateful marriages; young men are capricious or unfaithful. Passionately pursuing their dreams, these women weep often; but their tears dry quickly. Pretending obedience to gain time they swoon, simulate madness, threaten suicide, flee from home as servants or soldiers, drink sleeping potions, are buried as dead. They threaten death to successful rivals and ruin to men who spurn them. Some are constant; many are fickle; others change their love for gold.

Colombina, Olivetta, Rosetta, Fioretta, are serving maids; partisans of their mistresses and their lovers, they carry messages and make appointments. Living in an atmosphere of love, languor and intrigue, they fall in love early or else, hoping for marriage, they give themselves to old men. Sometimes they supplant their mistresses. They fight with rivals

COVIELLO (1550)

and pull hair. Lively, talkative, with smiles, airs and graces they pass across the scene.

In the improvised comedy the male actors are lovers, old men or servants. Flavio, Orazio, Florindo, Lelio are lovers; Sireno, Corinto, Selvaggio are shepherds; Adrasto, Corebo are princes. They sing serenades, threaten rivals, sometimes marry. Often they make love to married women, sometimes tempt young girls; and when jealous they seek to kill both rival and unfaithful fair. Disguised as beggar, doctor or notary, they enter the house of the beloved; and their amours are aided by clever servants.* The servants are called Zanni; sometimes Zan Ganassa, Zan Farina, Zan Capella; or named Arlecchino, Pedrolino, Frittellino, Truffaldino, Brighella, Pulcinella, Coviello. These servants love the serving maids and this complicates the plot. Jailers, beggars and innkeepers have the same names and practice the same roguery as the serving men.

In the *Commedia dell'Arte* the basic types are Pantalone, Dottor Graziano, Arlecchino, Pulcinella and Brighella; each of these characters having been made celebrated by some distinguished actor and becoming traditional as other actors assumed that name and the peculiar characteristics of that mask.

These strolling players are petted, receive rich gifts; yet often they are hungry. One authority protects them; another persecutes them. The public applauds and derides. Actors friendly on the stage quarrel behind the scenes. Today they live in luxury; tomorrow they wheel their barrows along

---

* In the ancient Italian comedy the lover was just a lover—usually a comic lover—his rôle played by the principal actor of the company; Flavio was the lover's name even before the appearance of Flaminio Scala. Ruzzante's Flavio is thus described by his rival Polidoro, "Because he is beautiful, gallant, a maker of sonnets, because he understands music, has court manners and dresses like a Spaniard, Flavio imagines that he can hold the love of Fiorinetta."

country roads, having been expelled in disgrace from some city. Tristino Martinelli received affectionate autographed letters from Queen Marie de Médicis; royal gifts, honours and offices were his. Drusiano Martinelli refused the Grand Duke of Tuscany's "two or three thousand scudi in cash," demanding "ten thousand all at once, besides my keep." The Queen of France ordered that five hundred ducats be given the Fedeli Company and another two hundred be paid them monthly. She placed a collar weighing two hundred *doble* round Arlecchino's neck. A Prince seeing Tiberio Fiorilli act in Rome presented him with a carriage and six horses. Louis XIV was godfather to Domenico Biancolelli's child. Maria Cecchini was ennobled by the Emperor Maximilian, and Angelo Constanti was created a noble by Augustus II of Saxony.

Scholars praised the comedians. Garzoni wrote that "while the world shall last, while centuries run and times and seasons live, every voice, every tongue, every cry shall sound the celebrated name of Isabella Andreini." In 1611 a *Corona di Lodi* in honour of Maria Maloni was published. In 1608 a *Racolta di varie rime* was dedicated to Orsola Cecchino ("Flaminia"). Tristino Martinelli ("Arlecchino") called Marie de Médicis "gossip queen hen." He wrote to the Grand Duke of Tuscany: "I implore, beg, counsel and expressly command you upon receipt of this not to fail to do according to the orders and command contained in this and my other letter. . . . as you hold dear my favour do as I order and command, and happy you if you are able to fit in with my humour. Try therefore to retain my friendship, as I am resolved to keep yours through the ages and time without end." Tallemant des Réaux records that on Arlecchino's arrival in Paris he visited King Henri IV, and when the King rose Arlecchino sat in his chair and addressed the King as Arlecchino.

ITALIAN PUPPET BALLET

Behind these fictitious splendours of the comedians' life what misery, tumult and discord; what pride, presumption, vanity, frivolity and jealousy; what intolerance of authority and restraint! Confined within narrow limits, in closest daily intercourse, the passions of these actors became intense. In 1609 Virginia Andreini wrote to Cardinal Ferdinando Gonzaga:

Your Worship will have heard how I have overthrown all the triumph erected by Signora Flaminia. Her nose has lengthened downwards as much as it was proudly in the air before. She is hated by all Turin for her frenzied haughtiness in the love of Cintio, to her very great shame it is true. On this Your Worship will hear a hundred stanzas and forty sonnets by Cavalier Marino. You will certainly hear them, for I shall take care that they come to your hand. Please speak of her to the Ambassador; for you will hear the most iniquitous things. All the companies cry out upon her temerity and Frittellino's. They would have settled her before this if I had not come to Turin. I try to bear with this ugly humour but shall not for long."

Cecchini ("Frittellino") writes of Giovan Battista and Virginia Andreini: "God preserve me and my fellows from being with Lelio and Florinda. Florinda and her husband's intrigues and persecution have brought me to ruin and perdition." In another letter to the Duke he said: "Baldina must be excluded from the company then going to France. With secret art she kindles such conflagration in the company that it is impossible to live in the turmoil. . . . With Baldina we shall never do any good either in France or in Italy." Giovan Battista Andreini denied making love to Baldina, succeeded in imposing her presence upon his wife, and when Florinda died he married her.

The amours between actresses and noblemen and between

the wives of citizens and actors roused jealousy and impreca-
tions. In 1590 Conte Ulysse Bentivoglio thus described the
company of the Desiosi: "It is a brothel of infatuation between strumpets and scamps." Vincenza Armani was poisoned
in Cremona by "some rejected lover." Carlo de' Vecchi was
assassinated by actor Pier Maria Cecchini. Fortunately, however, these quarrels usually concluded with violent words.

Ecclesiastical authorities stormed against the corrupting art
of the comedians. In his *Comœdio-crisis* published at Viterbo
in 1637 Father Girolamo Fiorentini maintained that it was
mortal sin to witness an obscene comedy; and every comedy
was immoral that treated of love or secret marriage. The ecclesiastical censors of his manuscript affirmed that it was not
mortal sin to witness an obscene comedy if the spectator "does
not take pleasure in the obscenity, but only goes to satisfy his
curiosity or for enjoyment." In Milan Cardinal Carlo Borro-
meo would have forbidden all comedies and wished that the
wicked race of actors should be extirpated. Civil authorities
persecuted them. In Paris Parliament opposed Ganazza's
company in 1571 and the Gelosi in 1577 and forbade performances by Italian actors in 1588.

Capponi, Commissionary for Pisa, after having permitted
the Pedrolino comedians to act in that town forbade their
return because he had heard "such an outcry about the
amours of their women that serious scandal might arise."
Even in Venice, the "sea-sodom" as Byron called it, the mart
of pleasure for all Europe, the city of carnival licentiousness,
the Council of Ten opposed the comedians. In 1768 the In-
quisition thus permitted a dramatic performance:

This evening if the door open upon theatricals, but not if the
door open upon a brothel. Remember that you comedians are
people hateful to God but tolerated by the Prince to gratify the

"LA VITA DI PULCINELLA" BY DOMENICO TIEPOLO

people who take pleasure in your iniquities. You people easily lose your heads but the Magistrate will be vigilant if you err. Comport yourselves like Christians, even though you are comedians.*

In his *Piazza Universale*, Garzoni says:

No sooner have they made their entrance than the drum beats to let all the world know that the players are arrived. The first lady of the troupe dressed like a man, with a sword in her right hand, goes round inviting the folk to the comedy. The populace hurries to take places. Paying their pennies down they crowd into a hall where a temporary stage has been erected. An orchestra of tongs and bones like the braying of asses or the caterwauling of cats in February performs the overture. Then comes a quack-doctor's oration to his gulls. The piece opens; you behold a Magnifico who is not worth the quarter of a farthing; a Zanni who straddles like a goose; a Gratiano who squirts his words out from a clyster-pipe; a lover who acts like a narcotic; a Spanish captain full of musty oaths, a stupid foul-mouthed bawd; a pedant who trips up in Tuscan phrases; a Burattino taking off his greasy cap; a *prima donna* who yawns through her mumbled part with eyes wide open to the chance of selling her overblown charms in quite another market than the theatre.

The show is seasoned with loathsome buffooneries and interludes which ought to send their performers to the galleys. These profane comedians present nothing which is not scandalous. The filth falling from their lips infects themselves and their profession with foulest infamy. They are donkeys in their action, pimps and ruffians in their gestures, public prostitutes in their immodesty of speech. In everything they stink of impudicity and pique themselves by barefaced bawdry and undisguised indecency. In one corner of the piazza you will see our swaggering Fortunato and his boon companion Fritate keeping the populace agape with stories, songs, improvisations, dialogues. In another corner Burattino sets up his bray of brass. You would think that the hangman had got hold of you, to hear him yell into your ears.

When the burlesque prologue comes to a conclusion, Burattino's

* Nicolò-Maria Tiepolo, about 1778, quoted by Molmenti in his Essay on Goldoni, Venezia, Ongania, 1880, p. 68.

master puts in his appearance. It is our old friend the Doctor with his Bolognese jargon and absurd pretensions to omniscience. Near by is the Milanese quack, velvet cap on head and white Guelf feathers waving to the wind. He is telling Gradello the story of his hapless love. Toward evening the crowd of quacks, blind musicians and acrobats thicken. Here is Zan-della-Vigna with his performing monkeys; there Catullo and his guitar; in another corner the Mantuan merry-andrew dressed like a zany, Zottino singing an ode to the pox, and here is the pretty Sicilian ropedancer. The whole piazza is swarming with folk selling a powder and pill for every ill. Men eat fire, swallow tow, pull yards of twine from their throats, wash their faces in molten lead, find cards in the pockets of unsuspecting neighbours.

When the play was given in a theatre the nobles came on to the stage, made love to the actresses and walked about during the performance. Woe to the actor who objected. In 1609 Cardinal Giustiniano, Legate of Bologna, commanded that whoever ventured to impede the comedians directly or indirectly by standing in front of them while they were acting, by sitting on the stage or by cries and hisses, "shall receive three stripes of the lash or three months' imprisonment and a fine of a hundred scudi" and whoever "throws apples, nuts or garbage at the comedians, or brings printed sonnets to advertise them from the stage, or fights or makes other noise during the comedy, shall fall under the above penalties and also the penalty of five years at the galleys or one year in prison, or exile from the whole of the Legation for five years" and whoever "draws arms shall fall under the penalty of death."

Decrees, regulations and proclamations promulgated in Florence, Bologna, Milan, Venice and other Italian states during two centuries, attest persistence of these evils despite threats of severest punishment. An "Advice" from Rome in 1668 relates that many went "to the comedy of the public theatre . . . more to see the revels, intrigues, feasting and

other things done in the boxes than to see the above mentioned comedy." The nobles chattered, laughed, passed nois-
ily from place to place, obstructed the stage, spitting freely on
the heads of the spectators below; the plebeians making an
uproar with voice, feet, hands and sticks; taunting and insult-
ing the actors, and hurling upon the stage "lemons, oranges,
apples, pears, turnips and other similar filth."

The heyday of improvised comedy was the middle of the
seventeenth century. When invention was exhausted and the
art had frozen into the traditional masks Pantalone, Arlecchino, Brighella and Pulcinella still represented the qualities
and costumes of the ancient Italian peoples; just as the Lelios,
Ottavios and Florindos with enormous powdered wigs and
laced shirts typified the more recent corruption. Such troupes
of professional performers passed from city to city; and in
popular theatres or upon improvised stages in the city squares
represented more modern versions of old farces and scenarios,
in which Arlecchino distributed blows, and the only season-
ing was lascivious gestures, indecent equivocations and vulgar
jokes; thus returning to the ancient tradition of mountebanks, mimes, acrobats, jongleurs, circus clowns and rope
dancers. The *Commedia dell'Arte* had sunk to its lowest
depths.

Chapter IV

The Plot—The Scenario—Improvisation—Zibaldoni

IN THE first *Commedia dell'Arte* there were no Arlecchini
and Pulcinelli, but simply the same servants and old men and
young lovers and courtesans and Spaniards who had acted in
the erudite comedy but were now represented in more popular form, were more ridiculous, more mirthful, with droll
gestures, foolish *lazzi*, songs and dances. Improvised comedy,
however, contained a conspicuous literary element. In Scala's
"Scenari" madrigals were recited, Fidenzio's poetry was read,
songs were sung, Boccaccio's stories were told and French was
sometimes quoted.

Improvised and studied comedy had many types and subjects in common. Ariosto's *Suppositi,* the *Mostro* of Terence,
Plautus's *Anfitrione* and *Pseudolus* were reduced to improvised comedy scenarios, which were also derived from tragedies, *"sacre rappresentazioni"* and melodramas. Giulio Strozzi's
melodrama *Romolo e Remo* (Venice, 1645) was reduced to a
scenario "to be recited in the Teatro Nuovo." Giambattista
Andreini, Cecchini and many other writers of scenarios for
improvised comedy borrowed largely from the classical and
literary comedies.

When the actor had a serious part he used elegant metaphors and rhetorical artifices. When his part was ludicrous he
invented *lazzi*. "By *lazzi* we mean," says Riccoboni, "the actions of Arlequin or the other actor when they pretend fright

THE NUPTIALS OF THE HUMPBACK AND SIMONA,
SIXTEENTH CENTURY ENGRAVING

or make jests foreign to the plot of the comedy. It is this by-play invented by the actor which the Italian comedians call *lazzi*." [In *Arlequin Dévaliseur de Maisons* Arlequin and Scapin are valets, Flaminia is separated from her parents and reduced to absolute poverty. Arlequin complains of their sad situation and of his meagre diet. Scapin promises that he shall have everything he wants, and orders him to howl and shout in front of the house; Flaminia, attracted by Arlequin's cries, asks him what is the matter; Scapin explains while Arlequin cries out that he intends to leave her. Flaminia begs him not to abandon her and appeals to Scapin who proposes a way to relieve her misery. While Scapin is explaining his plan to Flaminia, Arlequin interrupts the scene with various *lazzi*. He pretends to have cherries in his hat which he eats and throws the pits at Scapin; he catches a fly, cuts off its wings and eats it comically. This kind of trick called *lazzo* invariably interrupts the theme of Scapin's discourse, but also gives him an opportunity to renew it with more force.]

President de Brosses wrote:

This manner of playing impromptu adds vivacity and reality to the action. In the theatre the gesture and inflexion of the voice blend always with the words; the actors come and go, speak and act as if quite at home. It is this necessity to act on the spot which makes it so hard to replace a good Italian comedian when unfortunately he happens to be absent. . . . Any actor can recite what he has memorized. A good Italian comedian not only improvises while he is acting but blends his own actions and words so perfectly with his fellow player and enters so immediately into the other actor's part that it would seem as if the whole thing must have been planned and rehearsed in advance.

In regard to these improvisations of the *Commedia dell' Arte* Evariste Gherardi says:

Italian comedians learn nothing by heart; it is sufficient for them to be informed of the subject just before they begin to act; and each actor gives his own interpretation to his part. This requires an actor of the highest ability. For he must not only be able to interpret his own part but he must so understand the words and gestures of his fellow actors that they will seem to have rehearsed their parts together.

Besides these *lazzi,* the improvised comedy was full of ridiculous phrases, gestures, disguises, *faux-pas,* epigrams and cudgellings. The ludicrous was often founded on the indecent; women sometimes appeared naked on the stage. With the prevailing obscenity of the written comedy lewdness was inevitable in the *Commedia dell'Arte* troupe, which was frequently composed of mere mountebanks and low comedians. Of a drama only the outline (the *canovaccio* or *scenario*) was traced; the actors improvised the rest and that *rest* was everything. At each performance the dialogue was improvised afresh. A word, a gesture of the actor could suggest a repartee; the presence in the theatre of a gentleman friend or of a lady —who was not a lady—could inspire them with a piquant allusion. Every actor was an extemporary poet.

To succeed in the *Commedia dell'Arte* the comedian must have fertile imagination, facility of expression, extensive learning and his memory stocked with phrases, love speeches, expressions of despair on which he might draw when occasion rose; and he must know the language so thoroughly as to handle it with ease. Niccolò Barbieri said "Out of ten who try to recite, nine do not succeed," and Riccoboni writes "that it is easier to form ten actors for the regular comedy than one for the improvised comedy." Plays that are gay gain much with improvisation. There is a sparkle and truth in a spontaneous dialogue like the coruscation of fireworks. Each uses

SCAPIN (1716)

the expressions most natural to him, and if the actor is well educated his style will be elevated and correct. It is personality which makes for success or failure in improvised comedy; and in order to excel it is necessary to have a vivid and rich imagination and to express oneself fluently. The best improviser will give warmth to his play without forgetting the details and be careful to note what the others are doing or saying in order to provoke the reply that he needs.

Impromptu comedy has graces unknown to the written play. So great is the variety due to the moods and temperaments of the actors that one may see a scenario many times and each time it will be a different play. The impromptu actor feels more keenly and therefore speaks better what is his own than what he has borrowed from others through memory. But these advantages in impromptu comedies are limited by many inconveniences, since the impromptu of the best actor may be entirely ruined if he fails to receive the proper support of the one to whom he is speaking.

The Scenari of the *Commedia dell'Arte* were attached to the walls behind the wings. Perucci has explained how the comedians agreed upon the plot. "The *Corago*, or leader, should decide beforehand on the subject so that the plot and the limits of the speeches may be known. The leader must read the plot and explain the characters by name and characteristics; expound the argument of the story, the place where it is staged; fix the entrance houses, interpret the jokes and all the smallest details, in fact look after all the items necessary for the comedy." He will, for example, say: "The comedy to be represented is . . . the characters are . . . Then he will give the argument." "The actors must never forget the town where they are supposed to be and why they are there, and never fail to remember their names. It is

unpardonable for one to say he is in Rome and for another to say they are in Naples; that one coming from Spain should say he comes from Germany; for the father to forget the name of his son, or the lover that of his sweetheart."

The *Corago* interprets the jokes and the plot, saying: "Here there is to be such a jest, there such an equivocal scene; here such a metaphor, or bit of irony. He must be ready to remedy every difficulty that the characters may suggest." "Do not wander too far from the subject lest it be too hard to find the way back, and the audience lose the thread of the plot or fail to understand it. The actors should all assemble to listen to the instructions and not trust to their memory or to have recited the comedy before; for various leaders might agree on changes in the plot or on different names and places. Everything said, whether serious or ridiculous, must be introduced naturally. If night is to follow some scene be sure to mention it in the previous scene, saying: 'It is already night and thus comes dawn and brings the day.' "

Each actor in the *Commedia dell'Arte* had his own *zibaldone* (commonplace book) in which were collected hundreds of phrases, jests and speeches which could be adapted to almost every play. Pantalone had his *"Consiglio";* the Doctor, his *"Tirata della Giostra"*—a long list of ridiculous names and ludicrous discoveries; the Capitano, his *"Bravura Spagnyola."* The more expert actors while drawing phrases from the rich storehouse of their memory gave their discourses such *brio* as to make them appear scenes from real life. Hence it was natural that each actor should specialize in the interpretation of a definite character, assuming the type and pouring into it his own spirit. Francesco Andreini became Capitan Spavento; Fabrizio de Fornaris, Capitan Coccodrillo; Silvio Fiorillo, Capitan Mattamoros; Girolamo Garavini, Capitan Rinoce-

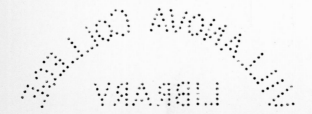

ronte; Giuseppe Bianchi, Capitan Spezzaferoo; Bianchi, Lombardi, Romagnosi are recorded as interpreters of the mask of the Dottore (Doctor); Benotti, Arrighi, Riccoboni were famous Pantaloni.

The complications of the "scenari" or love-plots of the *Commedia dell'Arte* are numberless and constantly changing. To feign death a sleeping draught is taken. To carry out her love intrigues a woman pretends to be dumb and possessed of evil spirits, the lovers and servants also feigning to be mad. Evil spirits appear on the stage and threaten, cudgel or carry off someone. In the *Commedia dell'Arte* the changing of clothes is a common artifice; Isabella, Franceschina and Flaminia dress as men; Fabrizio dresses as a woman; Arlecchino as a dentist; Flavio as a physician; Flaminio as a gypsy woman. Scenes of tumult, flight and confusion are a characteristic of the *Commedia dell'Arte*. In *Fortuna di Flavio*

Arlecchino the charlatan arranges the bench on which he is to mount and sell his goods; the *servitori* place his chair and valise on it; his companions come from the inn and stand on the bench. Turchetto plays and sings; Flaminia comes to the window and watches the players; Burattino listens; Franceschina looks on; Pantalone arrives and salutes Orazio. Gratiano praises his goods; Capitano salutes Flaminia and, recognizing Arlecchino as the man who has taken his sweetheart, pulls him off the bench; Orazio and Capitano fight; Arlecchino flees; Capitano flees; and in the midst of this uproar the bench falls over. Everyone flees into his own house, Orazio, Pantalone and Pedrolino following.

The *Commedia dell'Arte* deliberately chose the obscene, the unusual and the absurd. The unusual is sometimes combined with the spectacular as when the moon is seen all stained with blood or a soldier appears with the head of a murdered man in his hand; or a child riding astride a bear and leading a lion on a leash; infernal spirits, dwarfs with lighted torches.

In the *Commedia dell'Arte* Isabella is a coquette, an intrigante, a dangerous woman; near cousin to the Columbine adventurous type. She says:

The deplorable state of gallantry today requires that some woman should sustain the cause of her sex; we have too long waited for an avenger. Women have ceased to please; against certain stupid and brutal pleasures love has not held its own with the young men. The profanation of our charms in continually uniting us to imbecile old men has been a great enemy of gallantry; for they are a class despised by the whole wide empire of lovers. This strange alliance between youth and old age which avarice has suggested to our fathers permits many abuses. It causes separations and is the opportunity of elegant and dissolute abbés who are always on the watch for such incompatible marriages.

Girls do not willingly accept the rewards of such marriages; or when accepted, they hate the austerity demanded by spectacled husbands. Children and old people make poor soldiers of hymen. Imagine an old graybeard marching under the banner of love! Picture a young girl living with a husband who questions her every hour, counts her every step, is always contradicting her and boasting of his early prowess! A crabbed, surly old man who hates to see a new ribbon in her hair; who bribes servants to spy on his wife's most innocent actions. And what shall I say of the legion of maladies characteristic of old age, those insupportable coughs, the common music of an old man. It is true that I find something heroic in the courageous fidelity of those who support such husbands; but for myself I hate an old man who dares to restrain my liberty.

The Doctor rôle was first played by Lucio (1560). He is the *Pedante* of the Erudite Comedy. He is a savant, lawyer, physician, philosopher, rhetorician or diplomat; a chattering, conceited ignoramus. He spouts Bolognese dialect interlarded with Latin quotations and grotesque etymologies. Whether named Graziano, Prudentio, Hippocrasso or Balanzon, his learned imbecility matches the Captain's warlike adventures

SCARAMUCCIA (1645)

and amorous conquests. Akin to Doctor Graziano is the Biscegliese Pancrazio or Neapolitan Cucuzziello, the Cassandro from Siena or Facanappa from Venice.

Neapolitan Scaramuccia comes under the class of the Captains. His costume is black. Riccoboni says that this black dress imitated the Spanish costume used by the magistrates in Naples. A boaster and coward, he masquerades as a marquis or lord of various imaginary countries. Like his father the Capitan he falls in love promiscuously, boasting of favours, and slanders the women who refuse him. Pretending enormous wealth, he is usually the valet of some small lord or poor citizen. Scaramuccia is a rascal who delights in making trouble.

Taberio Fiorilli, one of the most celebrated Italian actors of the seventeenth century, was born at Naples in 1608 and died in 1696. Angelo Constanti, author of *La Vie, amours et actions de Scaramouche,* says that Fiorilli was the creator of the Scaramouche masque. Nature had miraculously endowed him with gifts for the part, and he was soon accepted in all Italy as the most perfect mime of all time. Scaramouche after putting the room in order sits down in an easy-chair and plays his guitar. His master Pasquarelli comes in and beats time over his shoulders. In a scene of pretended fright without uttering a word Scaramouche kept the laughter going for a quarter of an hour. A great prince seeing him play in Rome said, "Scaramuccio does not speak but he says a great deal," and when the comedy was over presented him with a coach and six horses. In Paris in 1640 Fiorilli equalled his Italian success. Every evening he came to the royal palace with his dog, cat, monkey, guitar and parrot to amuse the dauphin, afterward Louis XIV. He became a favourite of Louis XIV, and died in 1696 when eighty-eight years old. Molière greatly admired him.

Pulcinella is the Roman Maccus; the Maccus of crooked nose, long legs, humpback, big stomach; of absurd gestures, cries and funny speeches. About 1620 Pulcinella was introduced by the Neapolitan Silvio Fiorillo at Naples. Of Fiorillo's Pulcinella, Cecchini says: "This delightful man has introduced disciplined stupidity, at the first appearance of which melancholy flies away. I call it 'disciplined stupidity' because much study has been given to show a dolt little better than a madman, and a madman who frequently comes near to being wise." He adds that Capitan Mattamoros invented this super-stupid part. The name Pulcinella (from *pulcino,* an unfledged chicken) well suited this mask with round eyes, hooked nose and something of the fowl about him. Riccoboni says "in Neapolitan comedies the Brighella and Arlecchino parts are taken by two Pulcinelli—one sharp, the other stupid. Whether innkeeper, peasant, soldier, thief, rich man, father or adopted son, according to the part he is playing, Pulcinella is always a Neapolitan. About 1630 Pulcinella became a marionette; in 1649 he had his own theatre in Paris ("Je suis Polichinelle qui fait en sentinelle à la porte de Nesle"); and he became a favourite character in the suburban theatres of Paris.

In Rome and Naples, Pulcinella is still a great favourite. In his long loose white jacket and pantaloons, his beaked mask and whitened face Pulcinella intrigues, brings lovers together, creates *imbrogli,* laughs at his victims. Married; his wife and mother-in-law always quarrel. In one play Pulcinella while fighting with the devil fiercely pulls his tail. It comes off in his hands; he is amazed, makes extraordinary grimaces, smells it; and the odour is uncommonly good. He slices off and eats a piece. Another slice and another until he has eaten up the whole tail.

BRIGHELLA (1570)

The following passage from *Maridazzo di M. Zan Frogno-
cola con Madonna Gnigniocola,* printed in 1618,

> Tognaz dances with Bertolina;
> Brighella dances with Franceschina;
> The wenches dance with their beloved
> And the bride dances with her spouse,

is the earliest record of the Brighella mask. Brighella's first
costume was a coat with large pantaloons of white cloth, a cap
bordered with green stripes and a cloak. The coat and the
pantaloons were striped on the seams with pieces of green
cloth, a sort of livery. He wore a brown mask with a beard.
His modern costume is a white frock coat with three bands, a
vest and pantaloons also white and striped with green. He
preserves his traditional white cap bordered with green, his
brown half-mask, beard and light moustache, and looks something like a negro clothed in an absurd livery.*

Giuseppe Angeleri, a celebrated Brighella, played in Goldoni's comedies. Atanasio Zanoni of Ferrara, another famous
Brighella, was one of the best comedians of the eighteenth
century. He joined Antonio Sacchi's company and married
his sister; his pronunciation was beautiful and his repartees
brilliant. He was drowned in Venice in 1792. He said: "One
ought not to say a thief but a clever mathematician who finds
a thing before its owner knows he has lost it." "Things appro-
priated are property inherited before the death of the owner."

---

* Brighella is a liar, drunkard, cheat, dancer, musician, thief; sometimes an
assassin. A scorner of everything that is good and pure and true, he has many needs
and requires much money. With honeyed tongue and prepossessing manners and
fawning politeness, Brighella is an infamous scoundrel. Insolent with women, he is
a braggart and brawler to the old and helpless; yet he grovels and hides before those
who despise him. He fears you and hates you; Brighella gave that stab in the dark.
He prefers to serve those who are in love. When he works for himself God help the
girls who trust him; they are lost forever. Such was the original Brighella. The
modern Brighella has slightly improved; he murders less frequently; is more sly but
less violent. His only desire is to steal.

"To steal properly requires the aid of three devils; one teaches you how to take things without being found out, another shows you how to hide them so that they cannot be discovered and the third persuades you to never return them."
"When I am forced to travel, that is to say, to fly; I caress the widowed chickens, adopt their babies and the orphan ducks; I free the purses and watches from their captivity; I am a great talker because my father was dumb and has left to me an enormous number of new words which he never used. Also I am a bastard. My shirt is a romance full of wandering soldiers; and no one will wash it for fear of soiling the river. My debts make me a star never seen except at night. I am so occupied with my affairs that I have not even time to scratch myself."*

Mezzettino (half measure) originated in the Gelosi Company. He wore the clothes, masks, hat, tabarro and wooden sword of the ancient *zanni* as represented by Callot. Angelo Constantini was born at Verona, came to Paris in 1682 and first appeared in *Harlequin Proteus*. He entered the Gelosi Company in 1682 to take the Harlequin part, the same as Dominico Biancolelli; but, the Gelosi not having the second Zanni or Brighella, he took that character, calling himself Mezzettino and wearing the costume which tradition assigns to the ancient *Sanniones*. It is said that Constantini in ex-

---

* Beltrame is another type of Brighella popular in Milan. The celebrated actor and author Niccolò Barbieri acted this part in France under the name of Beltrame. He came from Milan to Paris with Flaminio Scala and Isabella Andreini in 1587. After the dispersion of the Gelosi Company, Beltrame returned to Italy and joined the Fedeli. He returned to Paris in 1613 with G. B. Andreini and again in 1623. In 1625 he became head of his own company. The Scapino type of Brighella is a plotter, conspirator, boaster, liar and great favourite with the soubrette. Scapin is the French name for Brighella and has been made immortal by Molière. Callot in his *Little Dancers* represents the Italian Scapino of his period, clothed in ample robes like those of Frittellino, with mask and beard, a cloak, enormous feathered hat and wooden sword.

pectation of receiving a large gift, dedicated a play to the Duke of Saint' Agnan, and went one morning to the house of the Duke hoping to receive his reward; but the doorkeeper refused him permission to enter until Mezzettino agreed to pay him one-third of whatever gift he should receive from the Master. On the stairway the first footman also demanded one-third of his reward, and on entering the room, the valet-de-chambre demanded the last third of his compensation.

Nothing remained for poor Mezzettino, who ran to the Duke and said: "Ah, monseigneur, here is a play for the theatre which joyfully I have dedicated to you and for which I beg you to give me a hundred strokes with your cane." The amazed Duke asked the reason for this singular request. Mezzettino replied: "It is, monseigneur, because in order to approach you I have been obliged to promise your doorkeeper, your footman and your valet-de-chambre, each one a third of that which you will be so kind as to give me." The laughing Duke reprimanded his servants and sent a hundred louis to Mezzettino's wife, to whom nothing had been promised.*

The Capitano, with his enormous moustache, his plumed hat, originated in Athens and flourished in Rome under the Caesars. He has the characteristics of Plautus' Miles. Such are Rabioso in the *Travaglia of Calmo,* the Zigantes in the *Alchimista* of Bernardino Lombardi. In Italy, Spain, France and England under different names he played a hundred rôles. This Cinquecento character remained popular through most of the seventeenth century, and was made famous by Fran-

* The Mezzetin of Gherardi's theatre has softened manners but is still the old rascally Brighella. Sometimes Mezzetin sings, accompanying himself on the guitar. Watteau has so painted him in the midst of the principal actors of the *Comédie Italienne.*

cesco Andreini's Capitan Spavento dell'Vall' d'Inferno (Captain Frightful from the Valley of Hell).*

Speaking both Spanish and Italian the Capitano is ridiculous as a soldier-lover. His bravery is stupendous; innumerable women love him. Who dares oppose a man who has armed himself with "the Tower of Nembrotte as Cuirass, Mount Taurus as helmet," takes "the rainbow for his crossbow and the Labyrinth of Crete for his cloak and all the Pyramids of Egypt for arrows," who has mounted "full of anger and fury to the top of Mount Olympus, and with his "crossbowing" has riddled both poles like a sieve? In the Circus Maximus he killed two thousand Gladiators and four hundred lions; and seizing the giant Briareo "round the middle" threw him down "with such force and fury that the open earth swallowed him alive and gave him to Pluto for his Steward." †

The Capitano is always the bully, the wholesale killer. Isabella is angry with Flavio; Capitano asks: "Madam Isabella, am I to kill this one too?" He strikes right and left with his sword and flees as soon as he is threatened. When Pantalone "draws his pistol" he flees headlong, but when Arlecchino reproaches him he replies: "I just went to prepare the old man's grave." He thinks that by a glance, a nod, a word, he can win any woman. He winks at the courtesans, caresses the slaves, robs the honest woman; but in the end he is derided and mocked. Giangurgolo is the Calabrian type of the captains, always a great coward, an enormous liar, always

---

* Girolamo Garavani (Capitan Rinoceronte), Fabrizio de Fornaris (Capitan Coccodrillo), Silvio Fiorillo (Capitan Mattamoros) and Tiberio Fiorilli (Scaramuccia) were other famous Captains. In the eighteenth century the Capitano gave place to other masks, and later he reappeared in the Neapolitan Guappo and Roman Rogantino.

† Le Bravure del Capitano Spavento, divise in molti ragionamenti in forma di dialogo, di Francesco Andreini da Pistoia, Comico Geloso, Venice, 1624.

IL CAPITANO (1668)

penniless, always hungry; yet sometimes he would go days without eating for fear of receiving a refusal. Like Mattamoros he is mad after women.

Stenterello was a favourite in Florence and in Rome; and delighted audiences at the Capranica Theatre. The Tuscan Stenterello was introduced by the actor and comic writer Luigi del Buono, at the end of the eighteenth century. With his emaciated figure, long thin legs, cornered cap with tassel hanging down the back, with a vulgar and scurrilous wit, a wealth of coarse and clumsy quips and jokes, he represents the low-class Florentine. Stenterello's face is painted in streaks; a front tooth is wanting; he wears a tri-cornered hat, breeches and long-tailed coat. He derives his name probably from his excessive parsimony. When Florentines deny themselves food they live *a stento*. Hence Stenterello by his ludicrous efforts at saving convulses the audience. He would marry for money but despises love. To his mistress he says: "I would not leave you and lose the marriage for—for—for—*sette crazie*" (seven farthings). Sometimes he has a servant Stoppino (a meagre thin taper), whom he starves. It has been said that the Stenterello character is the most difficult mask to depict. "One becomes a Harlequin by practice, but one must be born Stenterello."

Pedrolino, the first Zanni, is an important *Commedia dell' Arte* personage. Like the *servo* of the Latin comedy he is an accomplice in the love affairs of youth and robs the old. He has infinite cunning. He invents the fiction of Pantalone's bad breath; disguises Arlecchino as a dentist and necromancer; masks the youths as ghosts, derides the Doctor, Pantalone and Capitano. He laughs at women, scorns his rivals, boasts his tricks, proudly professes his ruffianism. Sometimes Pedrolino is a learned servant. Isabella beats him and the others abuse him; but always he avenges himself and is the symbol of victorious cunning.

Pedrolino, Piero and Pierrot are the same personage; appearing first in the Italian theatre of 1547 in a comedy called *Pierro Valet,* clothed in a long white shirt with a straw hat and a club in his hand. His master orders him to carry a love letter to Isabella. He loses this letter but steals one from a letter carrier and hands it to Isabella, which is the occasion of a complicated plot. Molière adopted this character in his Don Juan. In Gherardi's theatrical pieces Pierrot is always a valet. Peppe Nappa is a Sicilian character, and except for his manner of dress he is of the same type as Pierrot.

Burattino is a celebrated mask of the Gelosi Company. It was about 1580 when he appeared in Florence and became so popular that he passed into the theatre of the marionettes. Francesco Gattiti in 1628 wrote a piece entitled *Le Disgrazie di Burattino*. In Flaminio Scala's scenarios Burattino is always crying; a glutton, coward and dupe; sometimes he is valet of Capitan Spavento, sometimes of Isabella, and sometimes of Pantalone. On the stage he makes *lazzi* which have no relation to the plot. In *L'Innocente Persiana* Burattino as valet of the Prince of Egypt is perpetually losing and finding his master. Elsewhere he is a letter carrier who loses his missives or allows them to be stolen, which discourages him.

Leandro is fresh and youthful, covered with ribbons and lace; and is the preferred lover of the beautiful Lavinia, of Isabella or of Beatrice. Corneille, Molière and other writers give him an attractive character. In the Italian theatre in 1694 Charles Romagnesi, renowned for his beautiful figure, played this part with great success. After the death of Romagnesi the rôle was transformed into a ridiculous personage

LEANDRO

under the name of Leandro *il bello*. And this is the Leandro whom we still find in the pantomime plays.

Tartaglia is a Neapolitan mask. A babbler, gossiper, stutterer and stammerer, he never can express his ideas; which makes him angry with others and with himself. "Tartaglia," says M. Paul de Musset, "is an extremely popular Neapolitan type. He represents the hot south; is exhausted with the climate, suffers from chronic ophthalmia, and is in a state not far from cretinism. Heavy cheeks, long nose surmounted with enormous blue spectacles, invalid manner and false pronunciation are his characteristics." In Carlo Gozzi's comedy of *Roi Cerf*, Tartaglia is a stammerer and stupid, but nevertheless he is Prime Minister in the land of Serendippe. He wishes to marry his daughter to his master the King, but the King loves beautiful Angela, marries her and becomes jealous. The imprudent monarch confides in Tartaglia, who loves the Queen and is furious on account of the King's marriage. Hence the play's complications.

The mask of Facca Nappa is a favourite character in marionette companies; his popularity at Venice equals that of the Biscegliese at Naples. Posters announcing the performance of a play always add, *con Facanappa* (*Pantalone spetier con Facanappa*, etc.). Every time he comes on the stage he is received with applause. He says whatever he chooses, and makes many personal allusions, employing popular expressions and manufacturing others.

Giandujo and Girolamo are the same character. At the Fiano Theatre in Milan, Girolamo speaking the Lombard patois plays the same rôles of peasant, coward and glutton that Giandujo plays in Turin and Genoa. In his *History of Marionettes* M. Charles Magnin says that Girolamo fills at Milan an important rôle in all the farces, parodies and little satirical pieces. In Turin, in that long and terrible melodrama *The Capture of Delhi,* Giandujo as aide-de-camp of an Indian sheik delights young and old by his Piedmontese reflections, sallies and jokes.

The Lombard Meneghino in its modern form is of literary origin; probably invented by Carlo Maria Maggi. Meneghino is a man of the people, impudent and boisterous, but prudent and shrewd. The personification of the Milanese character, he has good sense, good-natured irony, a good heart and makes himself liked. Meneghino (little Dominique) is sometimes valet, sometimes master. He derives from the Menego of Ruzzante, and from the Meneghino of Ariosto's play of *Lena.* Spoiled child of the Milanese, the hero of the Stadera Theatre, Meneghino's talent consists in crude stupidity. He stumbles against the walls and furniture, but never falls to the ground. The Neapolitans have a character resembling the old men of early Italian comedy; Don Pangrazio the Biscegliese, so named because he originated in Bisceglie, a little city not far from Naples where an amusing patois is spoken. Pangrazio Biscegliese in the tearful intonation of his home-town dialect, exhibiting the absurdities of provincial capitals, delights the Neapolitan. Like Pantalone he represents various provincial types, but always he is a miser and easily deceived.

From the time of Plautus on through the centuries the Colombina type of soubrette has varied little. Catherine Biancolelli, daughter of Dominique, was the most famous Colombina. Highly educated, beautiful, and with a soft and lovely voice, she had a great success on the stage. Colombina says to Isabella:

It is not necessary to carry coquetry to excess, but a small pinch of it makes a woman more attractive. How often have I heard my mother say that coquetry is like vinegar: too much of it in a sauce

TARTAGLIA (1620)

makes it bitter and when there is too little it is flat; but with just enough it rouses the appetite. So when a woman is a coquette at the expense of her honour she goes to the devil; when she has none at all it is worse.

In the modern pantomime Colombina is the daughter, niece or pupil of Cassandro. Her loves with Harlequin are continually thwarted; while rich and powerful Leandre is favoured. But her fairy godmother saves her, and despite the plots of Cassandre, Pierrot and Leandre she marries her beloved Harlequin. Molière's and Gherardi's theatre are contemporary but the Colombina of Gherardi is far superior to Molière's Dorine.

Narcisino comes from the city of Malalbergo between Bologna and Ferrara. Since the Bolognese Doctor spoke the educated dialect, in the seventeenth century the actor Ricconi created another character, who spoke the lower-class patois. Narcisino was most popular in Bologna. He only came upon the stage in order to perform various clownish acts which had no relation to the play itself; wearing a straw hat and long hair, in imitation of the peasants; clothed in a very large and striped jacket and breeches. Sometimes he carried a *tabarro* on his arm or a basket of fruit in his hand. He came between the acts and talked freely with the public from the front of the stage. He criticized the manner of the times and recited his pleasant adventures in the country suburbs.

The Cassandro character was created about 1580 in the Gelosi Company, under the name of Cassandro da Sienna. In this play he is the serious father while Pantalone and the Doctor are ridiculous personages. Chapelle was the most celebrated of Cassandros. He was short, fat; and his eyes which he continually opened and shut were crowned by heavy eyebrows. His mouth was always half open and he had elephantine legs. In the Roman theatre Cassandrino was a respectable citizen about fifty years old but still young and agile; powdered, with curled hair and elegantly dressed; always having irreproachable linen, clean stockings and polished shoes with silver buckles. He carried a light, three-cornered hat and wore coat and trousers of fine red cloth with a white satin vest. Of charming character, courteous, educated, elegant, he personifies the elegant *monsignori* and looks something like a cardinal. He is a favourite figure in the Marionettes.*

In the sixteenth century in Bologna a popular poet, Giulio-Cesare Croce, used to sing in the public squares of the life and adventures of Bertoldo. Later he printed his burlesque epic; and as the enthusiastic public bought his books, he was encouraged to add to his Life of Bertoldo that of his son Bertoldino. After the death of Croce, Camillo Scaligero composed a third volume containing the life of Cacasenno, son of Bertoldino. This series had an enormous success in Italy and these characters passed into the theatre; every troupe of actors in Florence, Bologna and Lombardy possessing them. The Bertoldino was most popular. It is a mixture of simplicity and rustic trickery. For three hundred years this character furnished many scenes in many plays.

If physicians were turned into ridicule in the Italian theatre the apothecaries were not spared. In the theatre of Gherardi they bear the most absurd names (such as Viscautrou, Cussiffle, Clistorel) and they usually carry in their arms their favourite instrument. In the Italian comedies the Apothecary

* Cassandrino is a superior Rugantino, with more pretension but less defiant. One is a satire on the nobility and the other the buffoon of the people. Rugantino (the growler) is always complaining of his fate, always maltreated, always bearing oppression with patience. He is short, swaggering in a long dress coat, tricornered hat and wig, carries a sword; is always threatening to do great exploits, but in moments of danger runs away. Each of these characters speaks in the lowest popular dialect of his country—Stenterello in pure Tuscan patois; Pulcinella in the *Lazzaroni* Neapolitan; and Cassandrino in the Trastevere Roman dialect.

plays a considerable rôle in the plot and speaks of his art by metaphors and emblems. In addressing a Doctor whose daughter he asks in marriage, he says: "I am persuaded, sir, that a chair with holes in it indicates an apothecary better than a chair in which one is carried."

Chapter V

Some Further Scenarios and Masks of the Commedia dell'Arte

FLAMINIO SCALA gave the *Commedia dell'Arte* "the definite form with all good rules." Scala also published the first fifty scenari of the *Commedia dell'Arte;* the "teatro delle favole rappresentative ovvero la ricreatione comico aboscareccia e tragica divisa in cinquanta giornate." Scala's scenario of the Dentist is famous in the repertory of the Gelosi. Consider a few quotations.

Act I. Scene 1. Here Pantalone tells Pedrolino of the love he feels for the widow Isabella, that he suspects that his son Orazio is his rival, and that, fearing this, he has decided to send him away to college. Pedrolino reproves him taking the part of Orazio; they attack each other with words and blows. Pantalone, threatening, goes away saying he will speak of him to Franceschina the maid servant. Goes off. Pedrolino plans to revenge himself for the bite that Pantalone has given him.

Scene 2. Here Franceschina searching for Orazio by order of her mistress learns from Pedrolino the reason of the pain in his arm; in revenge they agree to pretend that Pantalone's breath smells bad. Franceschina goes into the house; Pedrolino remains.

Scene 3. Here Flavio (brother of Isabella) confessing his love affair to Pedrolino knocks against his arm. Pedrolino cries out; then they agree to pretend that Pantalone's breath smells bad. Flavio goes out. Pedrolino remains.

Scene 4. . . . Here the Doctor to whom Pantalone owes twenty-five ducats takes Pedrolino by the arm, who cries out and makes with him the same agreement about the bad breath, promising to

COMEDY PERFORMED FOR THE FIRST TIME
IN JULY 1694

COMEDY BY LOSME DE MONTCHESNAY
PERFORMED DURING DECEMBER 1693

COMEDY BY GHERARDI PERFORMED FOR
THE FIRST TIME IN OCTOBER 1695

ONE-ACT COMEDY PRODUCED IN
JANUARY 1695

FOUR COMEDIES

get him his twenty-five ducats. Doctor goes out. Pedrolino goes to find Orazio.

Scene 5. Here enters Captain Spavento, who boasts of his love for Isabella and his bravery. Here Arlecchino the servant of Isabella acts a comic scene and goes in to bring Isabella out. Captain waits. Flaminia, daughter of Pantalone, from her window sees the Captain and begs for his love. In this Isabella comes out expecting to find Orazio. Captain begs her love; she drives him away and he does the same with Flaminia, making a triangular duel. In the end Isabella goes into the house repulsing the Captain. He does the same with Flaminia and goes away. She remains disconsolate.

Scene 6. Here Pedrolino, who has secretly heard all, threatens to tell her father; then they agree about the matter of her father's breath. She goes in. Pedrolino, whose arm hurts him more than ever, wants to revenge himself at all costs.

Scene 7. Here Arlecchino arrives. Pedrolino bribes him with money to pretend to be a dentist. He sends him to disguise himself; Arlecchino goes out; Pedrolino remains.

Scene 8. In this Orazio understands from Pedrolino of his father Pantalone's rivalry for the love of Isabella, and that he intends to send him away to college; Orazio, sorrowful at the bad news, appeals to Pedrolino who promises help; and they agree about the matter of the father's bad breath. Orazio wishes to talk with Isabella. Pedrolino calls her. Isabella learns of Orazio's love and of his coming departure. She is distressed by it. Enter Pantalone talking loudly. Isabella hearing him goes in. Pantalone sees his son, whom he orders to go and get ready immediately, because he is sending him to Perugia. Orazio very timidly goes in to get ready, giving a look to Pedrolino. Pantalone is telling Pedrolino how he has spoken with Franceschina, when Pedrolino says: "Ohibo, master, your breath smells outrageously!" Pantalone laughs at him. Then Franceschina does the same, saying that if his breath had not smelt Isabella would love him, and she goes in. Pantalone wonders. Then Flavio passes and at a sign from Pedrolino acts in the same way to Pantalone and goes off. Pantalone is surprised. In this scene the Doctor arrives. Pedrolino makes a sign to him about the breath. The Doctor does the same as the others and goes off. Pantalone wants to ask his daughter if it is true about this. He calls her. Flaminia confesses to her father that his breath smells vilely and goes in. Pantalone and Pedrolino remain.

Scene 9. Orazio from the house confirms the same thing, then returns into the house. Pantalone resolves to have out the tooth which causes the bad smell. He orders Pedrolino to bring him a dentist and goes in. Pedrolino remains. Arlecchino appears dressed as a dentist. Pedrolino orders Arlecchino to pull out all Pantalone's teeth, telling him that they are decayed. Goes out. Arlecchino under the window cries, "Who has decayed teeth?" At that Pantalone calls him from the window. Then comes out. Arlecchino pulls out his instruments, which are smith's irons, naming them ridiculously. He makes Pantalone sit down and with the pincers pulls out four good teeth. Pantalone owing to the pain, catches hold of the dentist's beard which, being false, remains in his hand. Arlecchino runs away. Pantalone throws the chair after him. Then, bemoaning himself with pain goes into the house. And here the first act finishes.

Stupid and silly as this may sound to the modern reader, he should remember that it is but the attenuated plot; the filmy web of an embroidery which by those who saw it was extolled for the exquisite variety, vividness and contrast of its colours. In fact every scenario in comparison with its performance is something less than a skeleton. Where, for example, in another play it simply says, "Captain Spavento boasts of his love for Isabella and his own bravery," Francesco Andreini in his performance began one of those monologues which were of themselves enough to secure the success of the play and which the skillful actor developed in writing and gave to posterity under the title of *Le Bravure di Capitano Spavento divise in molti ragionamenti in forma di dialogo* (Venice, 1624). These *Bravure* are extravagances, exaggerations, blunders, devised and fitted together by a vaunting coward who knocks the bottom out of Hell, yet runs from every danger and is beaten by Arlecchino. Reading these scenarios today we miss many allusions and we are not able to see the tricks nor hear the voices of those players who were masters of acting.*

Even in private life actors used the stage appellations, sometimes adding their own family names. Whoever wished to represent the old Venetian, the Bergamese servant, the Bolognese pedant or the Neapolitan peasant, called himself *Pantalone, Brighella, Arlecchino, Doctor Graziano* or *Pulcinella;* dressed himself in traditional style; spoke the appropriate dialect with certain special inflexions of the voice. Thus the *Commedia dell'Arte* became static, the actors became marionettes and finally puppets were substituted.

In the *Commedia dell'Arte* the "Old Men" are Pantalone and Doctor Graziano. Pantalone is generally a good devil, frequently deceived by his children and servants. He descends from Senex of Plautus and Terence. Pantalone is often a glutton and sometimes an adulterer; frequents taverns and makes himself ridiculous with girls and widows. He is the old man who forgets his age but has all its defects and weaknesses. Doctor Graziano, the other old man, also is dissolute; but he is more ridiculous than Pantalone. The old men of the comedy rarely adopt habits and thoughts suitable to their age. Many are avaricious, blind, stupid and childish. They arrange marriages or prevent marriages. Meanwhile the youths and

---

* In his *History of the Italian Theatre* (1723) Riccoboni says: "This same Flaminio Scala had his Theatre printed. It was not dialogued, but only presented in simple scenarios . . . they explain only what the actor is going to do in the scene, and the necessary action and no more." The hundred scenarios of Basilio Locatelli and the scenarios of Domenico Biancolelli belong to the middle of the seventeenth century.

In the *Commedia dell'Arte* each actor so personalized his part that the rôle became himself, and other actors subsequently representing this character retained the original name, dialect, manner of speaking and dress of the actor who first had made the part famous. Or else they so completely altered these habits and manners as to strongly contrast the new and the traditional conception. In all Gelosi scenarios Flavio stands for Flaminio Scala; Capitano Spavento for Francesco Andreini; Orazio for Orazio Nobili; Isabella for Isabella Andreini; Frittellino for Cecchini, and the Neapolitan Silvio Fiorillo for the multiform Pulcinella.

the maidens and servants intrigue around them. Extremely
susceptible and led astray by love, these old men are imposed
upon in a thousand ways. They hurl themselves into desperate
adventures and resort to disguises and stratagems that com-
promise their dignity and reputation. Occasionally they recognize in the youth a long lost son, or in the maiden, a daughter long lamented as dead, and leave the field to their young
rivals.

The servants' masks multiplied enormously. Trappolino
makes love to his master's sweetheart and abets the son in
robbing his father; Francatrippa is always famished and frequently crippled; Trivellino is a mocker and a cheat; Far-
ganicchio, the small boy who is impertinent with women, a
glutton and idle—the true modern "gamin," who sings:

> Tirintina, tirintina
> Fusse festa ogni mattina!
> Ben da bevere e da mangiare,
> E poca voglia di lavorare;

> Tirilee, tirilay,
> If every day were a holiday!
> We would eat and we would drink
> And never work a single wink.

The cunning and stupid servants of the literary comedies
are represented in the *Commedia dell'Arte* by two *zanni* or
clowns. Cecchini affirms that "after the part of a shrewd and
clever servant, there should follow another so ignorant that
he fails to understand what is told him; from which pleasing
equivocations arise, ridiculous mistakes and other artificial
stupidities." Barbieri says that "the first servitor draws laughter . . . by his shrewdness; the second by his stupidities." The
zanni mask caricatures the Bergamese valley men who came
to the city searching for work. Pedrolino and Brighella repre-

sent the astute type of *zanni;* stupid lying Arlecchino is the other type. Burattino is a servant or merchant, half cunning, half foolish, who comes on to the stage with spit and urinal; Coviello is a Neapolitan mask with moustaches *à l'espagnol,* carrying in his hand a stick surmounted by an apple or an orange. And what shall we say of Mezzettino, Tartaglia, Scaramuccia, Pulcinella, Scapino and many another mask—each of these preserving the fundamental traits of character which were perfected by some actor! Traccagnino, Francatrippa, Coviello and Brighella might please the common public, but Pantalone, Arlecchino, the Doctor also pleased more serious people.*

Pantalone is sometimes husband, sometimes widower or old bachelor. Frequently he is the father of two troublesome daughters. Clothed in red pantaloons with Indian robe and cloth cap and Turkish slippers, he represents the old Venetian merchant busy with his affairs and mouthing orations, in the Piazza San Marco. He listens to every discussion and attempts to mediate when there are quarrels. Sometimes Pantalone is rich, clothed in velvet, and hopes to be a Doge. He has passed through many changes. When the play requires a virtuous man he is a model of hoary wisdom; when the plot requires a weak character he personifies the vicious old man made ridiculous by amorous quests. In the comedy *La Venetiana de sior Cocalin dei Cocalini* Pantalone is shown at his worst.

Arlecchino, the second *zanni,* is a liar, a swindler, a vulgar intermediary, his weapon the staff. He tumbles downstairs,

* In the Venetian *Commedia dell'Arte,* Tartaglia is the stammerer; Truffaldino, the Bergamesk caricature; Brighella represents the demagogues in the public squares and Pantalone is the bourgeois Venetian. Did his name come from *pianta-leone,* the "lion-planter" (since the early Venetian merchants who planted their Lion of San Marco banner on every Mediterranean island were jestingly called *pianta-leone*)? Or is Pantalone the San Pantaleone, ancient patron of Venice?

and upstairs, plays the charlatan "mounted on a bench." In
1776 Marmontel wrote:

Arlequin is the most bizarre and most entertaining character of
the theatre. A "Bergamesque" negro is absurd; it is possible that
an African negro served as the first model for this character. . . .
the costume of Arlequin follows that of the Latin mimes. . . . I
have found a book which shows the difference between that early
comedy and that of today. This character is a mixture of ignorance, wit, silliness and grace. He is a rough sketch of a man; a big
child with gleams of reason and intelligence, whose mistakes are
amusing. He has a cat's agility and his coarseness is only super-
ficial. He is the faithful, credulous, greedy valet, always in love,
always in trouble; who grieves, who consoles himself like a child.*

Arlecchino appears frequently in Flaminio Scala's plays.
His frights, beatings, falls reveal stupidity; he is malicious,
corrupt, fond of women, an expert swindler. As a magician he
distracts the Doctor's attention so that hungry Capitano may
stealthily eat seven fritters. He scolds Isabella for talking to
the Capitano whom he beats; snatches his beloved Franceschina
from Pedrolino; urges Isabella to dally with Orazio and with

* The etymology of "Arlecchino" is disputed. Some believe a *zanni* playing in
Paris in the time of Henry IV was under the patronage of an Achille de Harley and
called himself "Harlequino." Simone da Bologna was the *Arlecchino* of the Gelosi.
In the ninth century a French count Hernequin fought against the Normans, was
wounded and died in horrible agony in the Samer Abbey. Popular imagination was
impressed by his strange death and the desolation which his cruelty had brought to
northern France. Because of his sins God condemned him to wander with his companions until Judgment Day. Thus arose the Hernequin or Harlequin legend of a
wandering band of soldiers, which was soon fused with that other legend of the
cavalcata selvaggia, that ghostly band of lost souls galloping in the air during stormy
nights amid roll of thunder and noise of rain and wind. These wandering souls of
sinners, the Harlequins, afterwards became devils, and later on when they had lost
their diabolical perversity they became absurd; and in France as early as the twelfth
century they marched to the sound of many bells with a king of their own who was
the Harlequin or "Devil" *par excellence.* Later on real men, disguised as Harlequin
devils, covered their faces with grotesque masks, played on trumpets and abandoned
themselves to uncouth movements. In the late sixteenth century an Italian actor
performing in Paris assumed the name, donned the costume and presented himself
before the spectators as *Zanni Harlequin,* the Zanni who should surpass all the
others in extravagant buffoonery.

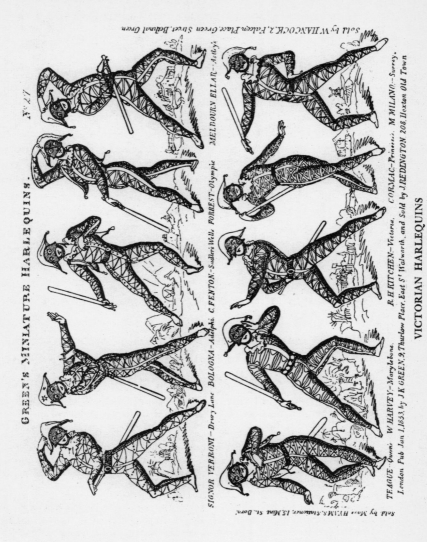

GREEN'S MINIATURE HARLEQUINS.   N° 27.

MELBOURN ELLAR.—Astley's   Sold by W. HANCOCK, 2, Falcon Place, Green Street, Bethnal Green

SIGNOR VERROCHT.—Drury Lane   BOLOGNA.—Adelphi   C. FENTON.—Sadlers Wall.   FORREST.—Olympic

VICTORIAN HARLEQUINS

TEAGUE.—Queens   W. HARVEY.—Marylebone   R. H. KITCHEN.—Victoria   CORMAC.—Princess   M. MILANO.—Surrey

London Pub Jan 1, 1853, by J K GREEN, 9, Thurlow Place, East S.t Walworth, and Sold by J. REDINGTON 208, Hoxton Old Town

Sold by Mess.rs HYAMS, Stationer, 13, Mint. St., Boro.'

"many other noblemen who love her," extolling the life of courtesans; and then when her husband appears, assures him that he possesses "the most chaste wife of the town." He swindles the Capitano and steals jewelry from the Doctor. Credulous, greedy, always in love, always in trouble, his absurd gesticulations, quick movements and sudden somersaults make his audience laugh. Arlecchino is the most disorderly mask of the *Commedia dell'Arte* and most resembles the mountebanks.

Joseph-Dominique Biancolelli (Dominique), the greatest Arlecchino of his time, was born at Bologna in 1640 or 1646. His father and mother were actors. From his early youth Biancolelli played in comedy with his parents and while still only a child he had become famous. In 1659 when Biancolelli was playing in Vienna in the company of Tabarini, Cardinal Mazarin requested him to join his Italian company of actors in Paris. Next year young Biancolelli came to France, and for eight years was the joy of the French court. King Louis XIV held his son at the baptismal fount. He was given the title of "King's Officer."

When in a fit of great mental depression Dominique consulted a famous French doctor, the physician said: "My prescription for your melancholy is to go and hear Dominique." "Alas," he replied, "I myself am Dominique and I am a lost man." Louis XIV's dancing master Sieur Beauchamp had danced a very singular and much applauded divertissement, in the presence of His Majesty. Dominique proceeding to give an imitation of Beauchamp's dance so pleased the King that he prolonged it until greatly overheated and perspiring. From this he contracted a cold, died on the 2nd of August 1688 and was buried in the church of Saint-Eustache. At the bottom of his portrait, painted by Ferdinand and engraved by Hubert, is written the following quatrain:

> Bologna is my homeland and Paris my abode.
> I reign there with lustre in the comic theatre;
> Arlequin under his mask hides Dominique, who
> Reforms with a laugh both people and court.

Here is an example of Arlequin's despair, taken from the play *L'Empereur dans la lune:*

Oh! unhappy one that I am! the Doctor wishes to give Columbine in marriage to a farmer and I will have to live without Columbine! No! I wish to die! Ah! Ignorant Doctor! Ah! Columbine so little constant! Ah! farmer much too much of a rascal! Ah! Arlequin extremely miserable! Let us hasten towards death. They will write in ancient and modern history, Arlequin died for Columbine. I will go to my chamber, I will tie a rope to the floor, I will get up in a chair, I will put the rope around my neck. I will kick the chair, and there I will be hung! (*He takes the posture of one that has been hanged.*) It is all over! nothing can stop me; let us run to the gallows . . . to the gallows! Fie, sir, what are you thinking of? Kill yourself for a girl? That would be great folly. . . . Yes, sir; but a girl to betray an honest man is great knavery. Agreed, but when you are hung will you be any the fatter? No, I would be thinner. No! I want to be of fair size!

What have you to say to that? If you want to join in just come along. Ho! no, indeed, you will not go. . . . Ho! I will go. . . . Ho! you will not go. . . . I will go, I tell you. (*He draws his knife, strikes himself with it, then says:*) Ah! now I am rid of that importunate fellow. Now that there is no one here, let us go hang ourselves. (*He pretends to go and stops short.*) Why, no! to hang is an ordinary death, a death one sees every day, which would not honour me. Let us search for an extraordinary death, some heroic death, a death that is Arlequinesque. (*He meditates.*) I've found it! I will stop up my mouth and nose, the wind cannot come out, and so I die. Done. (*He stops up his nose and mouth with both hands, and after having stayed in this position for a little while he says:*) No, the wind goes by the bottom that is not worth the devil. Alas! how laborious it is to die! (*Towards the audience:*) Sirs, if someone would die to serve me as a model I would be much obliged. . . . Ah! by faith I have it. We read in stories that some people have died from laughing a lot. If I could die laughing that would be a very funny death. I am very sensitive to tickling; if I were tickled long enough it would make me die of laughter. I'm going to tickle myself and that way I'll die. (*He tickles himself, laughs, and falls on the floor.*)

In 1689, Evariste Gherardi continued the Arlequin rôles, with great success. Constantine was the son of Jean Gherardi (Flautin) and born at Prato, in Tuscany. He made his first appearance in the revival of *Divorce,* in the rôle of Arlequin that Dominique had created the year before. His theatre was closed in 1697. He died suddenly in August 1700. According to his portrait he had a high forehead, large and keen eyes, aquiline nose, thin mouth and jaw.*

* See also in Chapter III of Marionettes, p. 117.

Chapter VI

Goldoni and Gozzi—
Decay and Death of the
Commedia dell'Arte

IN THE Piazzetta dei Mercanti in Venice, halfway between the
Rialto and the Merceria, close to the Riva where the daily
market was held, not far from the Piazza San Marco and
the bookshop where his friends and partisans met and but a
few steps farther from the Teatro di San Luca, now Teatro
Goldoni, is a statue of Goldoni slightly stooped as if listening
to the merchants and the shopkeepers discussing the day's
business or engaging in wordy warfare or banter, while
pigeons coo and flap their wings. If Goldoni could step down
from his pedestal he would find himself at home in this twen-
tieth century, and his comedies still being performed in the
Venetian theatres. Goldoni belongs to these people. Like his
own immortal Pantalone he was the synthesis of past centuries
and the forerunner of a new age.

This is the Goldoni who proposed to purge of its nastiness
while adding to its wit that degenerate theatre of which, in
the preface to his theatrical works, he writes: "The comic
theatre of Italy for more than a century past had so dete-
riorated that it became a disgusting object for general ab-
horrence. You saw nothing on public stages but indecent
harlequinades, dirty and scandalous intrigue, foul jests, im-
modest loves." In attempting this reform, Goldoni followed

the precepts of his time, was in harmony with the moral
standard of his environment, and did not attempt the impossible. His plays are the pride of the *Commedia dell'Arte* and
have become immortal.

Goldoni's plays glimpse every aspect of life, catch the spirit
of every social rank, show his love for the homely classes and
his condemnation of the Venetian aristocracy; though diverting episodes and amusing dialogue obscure sometimes the
courage of these attacks. The misfortunes of the humble are
not exaggerated, but he asks for fair play. Whether dissipated
husband, *cavaliere servente,* timid lover, spendthrift or gambler, most of his aristocrats are poltroons. The nobleman is
flattered by his wife's conquests, pleased to get rid of her;
but Pantalone, mouthpiece of the common people, abhors
such practices.

Goldoni's middle class are more chaste; wives are more
loyal, husbands more faithful. Goldoni's women are less
wicked than his men. Those modest, industrious young girls,
dainty Lucietta, Felicietta, who come and go so trim and gay
—playing their pretty pranks, pleading for their lovers or
plotting to captivate some grumbling old uncle—are truly
Goldonian. The wife, the mother are shown bravely protecting their family from ruin. When Goldoni's women are bad
their wickedness is an effect and not a cause. The coquettish
wife is the unhappy partner of a dissolute husband; the
peevish house drudge is embittered by long bullying. The
woman contrives and plots because her natural life has been
suppressed.

This thesis of the reform of society through the family and
by female influence was advanced in Venice, where public
opinion and the standard of morality was most unfair towards
women. Goldoni's little world praised feminine charms, wor-

shipped beauty with bows and compliments. But that the one half of mankind was the equal of the other was too absurd for discussion. Goldoni's rôle of the *servetta* is also significant. Goldoni's plays were crowded with healthy suggestions about the reform and the great influence of the family. He rehabilitated the most discredited trades and professions. He loved and understood the feeling and rights of the gondoliers. Goldoni defended the actors. He praised those who tried to live right, he castigated the individual but pleaded for the class.

Goldoni's inspiration, intuition and sincerity in depicting those humble people of the *calli, traghetti* and *piazzetti,* and in distinguishing their qualities from the aristocratic hand-kissing Lelios and Florindos, and his use of their vernacular, are unsurpassed. His *L'Impresario della Smirne* gives a pretty picture of theatrical customs. Admirable is his portrait of the physician who healed the spirit as well as the body. Lawyers he respected and admired. His *Avvocato Veneziano* is a hymn to the noblest calling. Most of his merchants are honest. Shop-keepers, tradespeople, even the humble *facchino di piazza,* pawnbrokers and money lenders find in him a defender. His scenes are few, vivacious, swift; but they are sufficient. The characters develop as the play progresses. We see frivolous girls in search of husbands, extravagant wives, infatuated husbands, adventurers, parasites, ignorant doctors.

Goldoni, most noted author of the *Commedia dell'Arte,* is a true Venetian. It is the intense sunshine and deep shadow, the *brio* and *amor* and *cortesia* of Venice which make the atmosphere of his plays. Vividly he describes his world. A marvellous observer, he is unable to generalize. He respects religious appearances. He does not invent his types but completes them through many plays. His female characters are many and varied; some of them are unsurpassed. He hates

militarism and loathes war. In his social plan, the family is the
nucleus of society.

In the long gallery of Goldoni's types, "Le Cortesan" is absolutely his own. What is a "cortesan"? In his *Memoirs* Goldoni says:

It is not possible to express the word "cortesan" by a French
adjective. The term "cortesan" is derived from courtesy or courteous. The real Venetian "cortesan" is honest, obliging, useful,
generous without profusion, gay but not foolish; he loves the
ladies without compromising them. He enjoys pleasure but does
not ruin himself in order to obtain it. He lives a quiet life but
refuses to be swindled. He is affable and is a devoted friend.*

Momolo thus expresses himself:

Money! Having it is not important, but knowing how to spend
it. A good cortesan gives the same value to his silver as to his gold.
He guards against stinginess, but will not be swindled. He can be
generous and when necessary can draw the purse-strings tight. He
is true with his friends, but with swindlers he meets trickery with
trickery. The world is full of cheating, deception is fashionable;
but I laugh at them for I always have a card for every play.

Momolo is placed in that most difficult position when a woman, a young girl, makes advances to him. Eleonora knows the

* This ideal of the Venetian "cortesan"—from whence did it come? And why,
before Goldoni, had the Italian comedy ignored it? Did Goldoni remember that
the poets of the *dolce stil novo* also had considered that *amor e cortesia* were
identical; that they had defined the laws of love and the code of courtesy and had
taught that honour should regulate pleasure and pleasure should be disciplined?
Always it had avowed that the art of living is the art of being happy, of amusing
and finding amusement, of being satisfied with oneself. The "cortesan" should
possess pleasing and showy accomplishments; should sing, recite, improvise, play
some musical instrument, give a serenade and pay his social obligation with something besides money. To be rich was not indispensable but to make a fine show and
at least appear magnificent and generous was important. Money might be borrowed
or gained by gambling—its source was not important; but it must flow freely
between the fingers, dance gaily on the green cloth or slip into the palm of some
pretty woman. Neither beauty nor youth was absolutely requisite, but gaiety and
boldness joined to a lissome body and a supple wit was essential to the "cortesan."

value of the love she has given to Momolo; and it is just because she is so deliciously pure that she tells him of her love, and proves it in a manner which will ruin her if she fails to win him. Of course, in the last act, Momolo accepts the marriage-chain and perhaps becomes a good husband. To complete the figure of Momolo we have the scene where, sword in hand, Momolo faces two assassins paid to assault him and persuades them to beat up their paymaster. It is a scene of repertoire, one such as the actors of *Commedia dell'Arte* have in their *zibaldoni;* but it is played with *brio,* gaiety and such good nature and irony that it would give pleasure today. The scene between Momolo and Ludro the usurer is delightful. Momolo's debt increases though he has made many partial payments. A rascally go-between demands an enormous percentage; spoiled merchandise is offered him in place of cash; all the other means familiar to usurers are described; but indignant Momolo gives the usurer his lesson.

How charming, how artificial, how piquant and naïve is the eighteenth century theatre type of soubrette; elaborated after ancient comedy traditions and long presented in comic opera and vaudeville. How gay her laughter, how keen her repartee, how knowing her smile, how sincerity is disguised by artifice! With her little cap balanced on black curly hair, little lace apron and bodice freely open at the neck, when her little slippers and lace stockings advance on the stage one realizes that in Colombina alluring youth, good sense, satire without bitterness, mischief without perversion, skill without trickery, kindliness without vice have entered upon the scene, to encourage bashful lovers, make fun of graybeards, sustain the rights of love and of youth against intriguing old age and selfishness. That darting repartee will pass over the heads of the dotards in the play but will reach the audience. Loose

COLOMBINA (1683)

talk, insinuations, will be exchanged but no actual grossness. Colombina is never wanton.

She has disappeared, this pert soubrette to whom one says everything, who understands everything and to whom everything is permitted. She has disappeared, this natty, lissome, pretty soubrette. She who could skim the brink of the abyss yet escape improprieties; could weave intrigue yet protect lovers; arrange the rendezvous but prevent the *finale appassionato*—she has disappeared as all artistic creations disappear with the changing humour of the public. In the *Commedia dell'Arte* she was always represented by the youngest and prettiest actress. Born in the mud of ancient cesspools, elevated by the pomp of improvised comedy, she illumined the comedy of masks. Each author transformed this supple figurine according to his own ideas. Goldoni found his soubrette already fashioned by the *Commedia dell'Arte,* but chiefly he found her among the comedians who were his first masters.

In his earlier pieces she was Colombina, the scandal-bearer, sower of discords. Aided by the collaboration of Mme. Baccherini, Goldoni soon evokes a quite different soubrette. In the *Donna di Garbo,* a comedy of transformations, the actress shows the whole range of her talents. A mere change of costume or headdress no longer suffices. In order to conquer an entire family there must be a metamorphosis of attitude, almost of character. Playing with the gambler, wise with the learned, attentive to the old grumbler, coquetting with some, austere with others, the "sly dog," the woman *di garbo* becomes at the end a sentimentalist. Goldoni never attempted to duplicate this rôle. In his other plays he placed Colombina among the subordinate characters. Realizing that the proverb "Like master like man" is doubly true in regard to women, he made his Colombina to fit rôles consistent with those of her mistress.

In *La Serva amorosa* he calls her Corralina and gives her a Goldonian and Venetian physiognomy. This adjective *amorosa* does not correspond with the French word *amoureuse*. It is not a question of love but of tenderness, of devotion, of active kindness and a chivalric impulse. Goldoni, connoisseur and interpreter of feminine souls, knew how to divine that heroism, abnegation, patience and fidelity which was hidden behind trifling manners or deliberate coldness, especially where the woman wished to save her little too sensitive heart, her little too punctilious *amour propre*. Corralina does not wear her heart upon her sleeve. She has reticences even from herself. Under her white purity of devotion there glows a little flame which, unless repressed, may flare into a conflagration. And it is this something understood, a martyr's aureole, which adds poignant charm to her person. Here are two Venetian bourgeois families, that of Pantalone, father of charming Rosaura, and that of Ottavio, father of Florindo. Ottavio is now the husband and slave of Beatrice his second wife, and is stepfather of Lelio. Florindo is maltreated by his stepmother, driven from home by old Ottavio; and but for Corralina he would have starved. It is Corralina who brings about his marriage with Rosaura, the recognition of his rights as the heir, and the banishment of the second wife and stepson. This dénouement complies with theatrical tradition.

Notice the difference between Goldoni's Corralina and Molière's and Marivaux's most famous soubrettes. How natural her introduction! She knits a pair of stockings. The yarn came from her dead mistress. "Ah, but those were the happy days. Patience! I have undertaken to help poor Mr. Florindo and I will never go back until I have finished that which I have promised to do. Poor Mr. Florindo! I love him as if he were my brother. My mother nursed him. We have both drawn milk from the same breast. We have grown up together and besides I have a very tender heart. When I have become attached to anyone, I would let myself be cut in pieces for them." Florindo enters the house weeping. He is penniless. Corralina gives him kind words and vague promises. She is only loaning him the money. "Yes, yes, I don't intend to give you a single thing. I am keeping count of everything. I will demand payment to the very last penny." Rosaura buys the stockings and listens to Corralina's gossip about Florindo's passion. Florindo is the pearl of young men. He never scolds, hasn't a vice, doesn't gamble nor run around with wild young men or girls, nor does he drink. Corralina also hints at the great expectations of this the only son of a rich father. She does not tell the whole truth but overflows with fantastic explanations. "Florindo has left home because he wishes to marry; he stays in this neighbourhood because he loves these windows, and very well you know why. In love with me? Don't be so foolish. He is a very serious young man and madly in love with you."

Having thus started the affair and drawn from Rosaura a half-confession, Corralina returns home and finds Florindo in despair. Madame Beatrice has ordered the notary to make Ottavio's will, entirely in favour of his stepson Lelio and of herself. Corralina says, "We will begin by having a good lunch; then I will talk with the notary." Pantalone enters; ensues a combat between two finished duelists. Two absolutely Venetian types are facing each other, and it is a treat to witness the rapier thrust. "Never enter my house," Pantalone orders. "I am tired of quarrels on account of Florindo; I am through with him and his family." Corralina blackguards him, pretends she has been personally insulted, appeals to his vanity. A fine man! With wealth and high position to tamely allow the insults of Madame Beatrice and of Ottavio to pass unpunished! Why, he should help Florindo! And what a splendid thing would be a marriage between Florindo and his daughter Rosaura! Florindo possesses every desirable quality himself. Very soon he will return to his family and take his own rank and he will make a brilliant marriage; probably to some little simpleton, one of the many coquettes hanging around, eager to catch such a desirable husband as Florindo will be.

Rosaura visits Corralina, Florindo being hidden in the next room. Corralina again discusses the virtues and the brilliant prospects of Florindo and promises that some day Rosaura shall come to her house to talk with Florindo since there is no other way to arrive at an understanding. "But if anyone should find out?" "No one will find out." "How shall I know when to come?" "Leave that all to me; only promise that you will come when I tell you to." The promise is made. Rosaura calls in Florindo and the classic *Commedia dell'Arte* scene is played between timid lovers and encouraging soubrette. Then before the powder explodes she intervenes. How many such representations are to be found in the *canevas* of the *Commedia dell'Arte* and in the *zibaldoni* of the actors! The making of Ottavio's will is amusing. Corralina accompanies the notary, and when Beatrice goes out with him she persuades Ottavio to realize his duty to his own son and to drive Beatrice and his stepson from the house. Corralina is Goldoni's most perfect soubrette. His others are pathetic and tearful or deceitful and tricky; what they gain in realism, they lose in charm.

Precursor of the moralists and psychologists of the following century, Goldoni discovers in the soul of Valentina, the housekeeper, the profound and ancient causes which explain the violent reaction against established order. Who before Goldoni searched for a soul in revolt lodged in the body of a soubrette? In what play before Goldoni's is there found such contrast between vice and greatness of soul as in this housekeeper who manages everything and is herself dominated by a rapacious sister, and by a lover of the lowest type? Other *Commedia dell'Arte* sketches present a woman trying to win an old man's affection that she may rob him for the benefit of her lover. But Goldoni shows a woman dominated by a blind passion which overwhelms all prudence, a madness which disregards all moral law. Her lover is unworthy but she loves him; her sister Felicita is a procuress yet she loves her; and she knows and judges herself for what she is. She is wicked because life has made her wicked; because "the hatred which I have breathed in has rendered me hateful, because in escaping vengeance I have undertaken to avenge myself." Utterly spoiled by the indulgent master, she has herself been conquered by love. Valentina is a milestone along the pathway of society's development; the servant who has become a thinking individual; a personality apart from other personalities in the vast sea of human passion.

Goldoni's personages are not to be found in the medley of Piazza San Marco; they have their own popular resorts, in some secluded *bottega* where they indulge in the sumptuous feast of a cup of coffee and a few crackers made of insipid flour paste.

In *Le Massere* Goldoni sketches an entire group of little maidservants. La Massera is a maid of all work. She has recently come from the country and has not lost the bright cheeks, the freshness of those gentle valleys. It is the maidservant of modest Venetian families, whose mistress has no secrets from her; or whose elderly master is sentimental and who to his fatherly affection for her adds a different kind of love; "but nothing, you understand, in the slightest degree improper." In the early morning these maids are on their doorsteps or their balconies, gossiping, calling or disputing for the favour of the handsome young fellow who visits the fountain, and offers to take them all to the coffee house. It is the last day of the Venetian Carnival and these gay young girls and even Donna Rosega, from whom age has not taken the lust of youth, have wandered freely with their beaux. What a day! What escapades because of their masks! What a whirlpool of little plots, unexpected meetings, of gaiety! What peals of laughter; bright sparkles as from a skyrocket!

How amusing the dialogue between old graybeards Biasio and Zulian—each recounting the charms of devoted servants, tender, attractive, affectionate, patient. "One who knows how to put her hand to everything," says Biasio, "and don't imagine for a minute that she is old. She is young and pretty—at least I find her so. What more could you want?" Zulian praises his own maid. "Agnes tells me that I look like a man not forty years old, and she ought to know." The other tells how she sees that he is properly shaved and assures him that he has cheeks like a rose and is as active as a young boy. One can guess what Goldoni would accomplish in bringing together these masked graybeards and servants. Jewels indeed are these pictures, yet are they rarely played. For where are the actresses to depict this type of soubrette? Such cleverness and gaiety! The world is too old, too sad for her.

The Mirandolina type of soubrette is no longer exactly a servant. She is the *locandiera;* she presides over a little establishment which admits only well known guests, where service becomes hospitality and where orders are requests for favours. It is a little middle-class boarding house with a mingling of bachelors' rooms. The Chevalier Ripafratta, the Marquis of Forlinpopoli, the Count of Alba Fiorita are permanently established here. Two of them already love her. The Marquis of Forlinpopoli, a finished type of the ruined and vain *barnabotti,* offers her a title of nobility and the half of his poverty. "The most excellent seignor Marquis wants to marry me. Ah, well, there is just one little difficulty," says Mirandolina. "I will have nothing to do with him; I like the roast but not the smoke. If I had accepted all those who wished to marry me I would have had many husbands. All those who come here make love to me, and they all end by asking me to marry them. It is not the same with the Chevalier Ripafratta. He makes himself out a countryman and acts like a bear; he is the first stranger who has come here who has not shown any pleasure in talking to me. He hates women! He can't bother to even look at them! Ah, the poor little fool! He will soon find one who knows how to teach him what is what!" Goldoni's Mirandolina shows exquisite delicacy; one word more or less, one gesture a little more bold and she would have glided into triviality or impudence. Experience has made her independent; pride keeps her from being too humble; but she is never a prude.

Pantalone is Goldoni's mouthpiece; he is also the central figure of the Goldonian comedy—the chief Venetian mask and best representative of the Venetian middle class. Goldoni found the character already fixed in the popular comedy. It was the mask the least masked. His tall figure, pointed beard, dark clothes, big cloak; his slippers, most appropriate for the few steps separating Rialto from Piazza; his supple gestures, measured tones, politeness, affable manner, long discourses, rough scoldings and facile gentlenesses; his cleverness in unravelling complicated affairs and his ability to make the best of good opportunities; his amiability to strangers; his complaisance toward his superiors—all this was as familiar in the city as in the theatre. Stationed in the *piazzette*, seated before the tables of the café Florian or grouped on the Rialto bridge, or in the evening filling the halls of the Ridotto, there were plenty of real Pantaloni such as one would see on the stage of the *Commedia dell'Arte*.

In the past he has been called "Magnifique," has been more cheerful. If he has aged and become more serious because of greater difficulties and smaller profits, it is because the magnificent Venice of earlier days has now become shut in and her commerce has dwindled. Life has become more complicated and it is necessary to be more industrious and clever. He becomes authoritative and dictates the law, he supplants the patrician, he becomes banker, lawyer, professor and even minister-of-state, replacing the formerly venerated patrician. Pantalone is prudent but not cowardly. He no longer fights duels, but he faces an insolent and will threaten those who affront him. In *La Putta Onorata* he says to Ottavio, "Monsieur the Marquis, go and give your orders in your marquisat." In later plays Goldoni's Pantalone becomes more clever and less aggressive; he has had more experience. The evolution of this character through Goldoni's plays and in situations always slightly different portrays Goldoni's finest art. In Goldoni's comedies the moral flows with perfect naturalness and spontaneity, and if there is not always a triumph of virtue there is always a logical triumph; that logic which regulates so many things and which explains so many others.

Carlo Gozzi was Goldoni's jealous rival. His *La Tartana degli influssi* is malicious. Even before Goldoni had started for Paris, Gozzi had won the applause of fickle Venice by presenting a fantastic drama constructed upon the lines of the old *Commedia dell'Arte*. On the evening of January 25, 1761, Antonio Sacchi's company with enormous success performed Gozzi's play *L'Amore delle tre melarance*. Once upon a time the King of Coppe's son Tartaglia was dying of ennui and consumption; his only cure was to laugh. A little old woman Fata Morgana appears and Truffaldino tips her over in a most humiliating manner. The Prince laughs loudly and is cured. In revenge Fata Morgana secretly inspires him to conquer "The Three Oranges." The Prince and Truffaldino undertake this strange adventure wherein alternate the phantasmagoria of the Spanish theatre and the heroics of chivalric romance. Venetian audiences were pleased that these masks which had come from the antique Roman mimes, had lived across the darkest ages, had impersonated Italian regions and races and had amused so many generations should continue to live on the Italian stage.

Gozzi writes:

I presented *L'Amore delle tre melarance* to Sacchi's company of comic players and the extravaganza was produced in the theatre of San Samuele at Venice during the Carnival of 1761. Its novelty seasoned with trenchant parodies of Chiari's and Goldoni's plays created such a sudden and noisy revolution of taste that these poets saw in it the sentence of their doom. Who could have imagined that this twinkling spark of a child's fable should have outshone the universally applauded illumination of two famous talents, condemning them to obscurity; while my own dramatized fairy-tales enthralled the public for many years?

In 1762, after having given *L'Amore delle tre melarance, Il Corvo* (The Raven), *Il Re Cervo* (King Stag) and *Turandot,* Sacchi's company removed to the larger theatre of San Angelo.

In his *Fiabe* Gozzi employed the four chief masks and the

Servetta Smeraldina. Because of Sacchi's talent Truffaldino's rôle was left to improvisation. Gozzi wrote out the dialogue of the other masks when he thought them sufficiently important. Stammering Tartaglia of the *Three Oranges* is still the Neapolitan glutton and knave. The Tartaglia of the *Little Green Bird* is the carnal careless boon-companion. Most of the *Fiabe* subordinate the masks, but sometimes they are important. A book of Neapolitan fairy-tales, *Il Pentamerone del Cavalier Giovan Battista Basile, ovvero lo Cunto de li Cunti,* largely inspired Gozzi's *Fiabe.* The novelty of Gozzi's plays secured audiences but failed to interest Italian readers; but to German and English critics Gozzi is the harbinger of Romanticism. His fantasy is the product of his surfeited memory. His plays were vulgar caricatures but they contained valuable motives.

The *Little Green Bird* is Gozzi's best play. Ninetta had given birth to twins, Renzo and Barbarina. The wicked old Queen-mother, pretending that these are only two spaniel puppies, ordered Pantalone to drown them and imprison her daughter-in-law Ninetta in a dungeon. The twins were not killed but were brought up by the peasants Smeraldina and her husband Truffaldino. Truffaldino has lately turned the children out of his pork shop and they wander in search of a home.

These children have been reading philosophy and they prattle philosophical maxims with as little comprehension as did Gozzi's Venetians. Renzo declares that the death of their parents has destroyed the normal human longing for family ties. Barbarina confesses that she is courted by a pretty little green bird. To the dungeon where Ninetta is buried alive the little green bird brings a bottle and a basket of food. To the audience he tells his own little story and the longer tale of Ninetta's woes. How Renzo and Barbarina are wandering on a desert shore, seeking distraction from their misery by talking of future good times. A speaking statue of Cadmon joins in the conversation, presenting Gozzi's own philosophical viewpoint. In the last act, everything comes right. Tartaglia is transformed into a frog, Brighella into an ass. King Tartaglia learns that Barbarina, being his daughter, cannot be his wife. His Ninetta is restored to him after her long captivity under the sewer. The little green bird becomes a royal Prince and marries Barbarina.

Turandot, written in verse and prose, has been widely praised. Its merit lies in the evolution of Turandot's character. When Calaf has won the prize Turandot cries out that she hates him and will die rather than marry him. Chivalrous Calaf answers that he will give the Princess another chance. If she solves his riddle his life will be forfeited. The riddle is to guess his own name. Adelma loves Calaf and, to prevent the marriage, discovers the name and tells it to Turandot. Calaf having lost lifts his dagger to pay the penalty. Turandot's love conquers her pride. She entreats Calaf to take her for his wife and obedient slave.

In none of his plays did Gozzi produce a true work of art. An ultraconservative devoted to the old aristocracy of which he was a part, all foreign ideas distressed and distorted his mental balance. Harbinger of Romanticism, reviver of the *Commedia dell'Arte,* he personified and agonized in the crumbling of the old aristocratic Venetian order.

I lay my pen aside just at the moment when I should have had to describe that vast inundation called the French Revolution, which swept over Europe, upsetting kingdoms and drowning the landmarks of immemorial history. This awful typhoon caught Venice in its gyration, affording a splendidly hideous field for philosophical reflection. The ululations of the dreamers yelling

out Liberty, Equality, Fraternity deafened our ears. I always
dreaded and predicted a cataclysm as the natural consequence of
those pernicious doctrines. Yet my Cassandra warnings were
doomed to remain as useless as these Memoirs will certainly be.

It was not by accident that Goldoni and Gozzi appeared at
the same time among a people who had not yet given full
measure to their genius in drama, comedy or tragedy. Under
a diversity of temperament and of literary accomplishment,
Goldoni and Gozzi have certain traits in common. Each of
them is utterly Venetian. The sum of their personalities and
of their writings presents a remarkable picture of Venice at
the close of the eighteenth century. Gozzi's rabid jealousy of
Goldoni and the enormous excitement which their contro-
versy produced in Venice seem almost incredible. It is im-
probable that it could have occurred in any other city or in
any other time. Hatred of Goldoni is Gozzi's master passion;
it is the inspiration of Gozzi's plays. It was more than a hatred
of personality. Gozzi loved all that Goldoni wished to destroy;
he despised the common people whom Goldoni loved.

In his Memoirs Gozzi writes:

We did not shun the theatres. We were not so unjust as to
refuse his share of merit as a playwright to Goldoni. We did not
confound him with Chiari to whom we conceded little. Yet every-
where tables, writing desks, booksellers' stalls, schools, colleges and
convents were filled with the trivialities and absurdities of both
quill-drivers; and everything these scribblers sent to press was
valued as a mirror of reform in literature, a model of right thinking and good writing. I recognized in Goldoni an abundance of
comic motives, truth and naturalness. Yet I detected a poverty and
meanness of intrigue; nature copied from the fact, not imitated;
virtues and vices ill-adjusted, vice too frequently triumphant;
plebeian phrases of low double meaning, particularly in his
Venetian plays; surcharged characters; scraps and tags of erudi-
tion stolen Heaven knows where and clumsily brought in to im-

pose upon the crowd of ignoramuses. Finally, as a writer of Italian, except in the Venetian dialect, of which he showed himself a master, he seemed to me among the dullest, basest and least correct authors who have used our idiom.

In spite of all the praises showered upon Goldoni, paid for or gratis, by journalists, preface-writers, romancers, apologists, Voltaires, with the single exception of his *Bourru Bienfaisant* he never produced a perfect dramatic piece. At the same time he never produced one without some excellent comic trait. In my eyes always he had the appearance of a man born with innate sense of how sterling comedies should be composed. He displayed an extraordinary ability for interweaving dialogues in the Venetian dialect taken down verbatim in the houses of the common people, taverns, gaming halls, traghetti, coffee-houses, places of ill-fame and the most obscure alleys of our city.

Audiences delighted in the realism of these plays. Never before had realism been so brilliantly illustrated, illuminated and adorned as it now was by the ability of actors who faithfully responded to the spirit of this new and popular type of farce. I maintained and proved that he had frequently charged the noble persons of his plays with fraud, absurdity and baseness, reserving serious and heroic virtues for personages of the lower class. I also showed that his "Putta Onorata" was not honest, that he had incited to vice while praising virtue. With regard to this point the four-mouthed Comic Theatre kept protesting that it wished to drive the time-honoured masks of improvised comedy off the stage, accusing them of imposture, immodesty and bad example for the public. I, on the other hand, clearly proved that Goldoni's plays were a hundred times more lascivious, more indecent, and more injurious to morals.

Gozzi also hated Pietro Chiari the Brescian, who had lived many years among the Jesuits and was titular poet of Francesco III of Modena. He was an elegant and worldly abbé, author of academic dissertations and of philosophic and scientific letters. The extravagant spectacular plots of his plays were heightened by abundant plagiarisms. His comedies were performed by the Sacchi and the Medebac companies. "A hot brain," Carlo Gozzi calls him in the *Memorie Inutili,* "disorderly, audacious and pedantic. When he writes for the theatre he has an astrologer's obscurity of plot, seven-league boots, . . . some good theatrical surprise, some stupidly happy description, . . . the most inflated and bombastic writer who has adorned our century."

The quarrel with Goldoni and Chiari, the alliance with Sacchi, the composition of the *Fiabe* and twenty-three plays on Spanish subjects, the liaison with Teodora Ricci, the episode of Gratarol, and the *Memorie Inutili* sum up Gozzi's life. The Republic of San Marco fell. Aristocratic Gozzi bowed to the French Revolution. His old age was passed in comparative solitude. When the old *Commedia dell'Arte* and the old actors died Gozzi's *Fiabe* were relegated to the marionette stage, where some of their scenari are still performed. Italy has elected to ignore Gozzi and to deify Goldoni.

The *Commedia dell'Arte* was the special glory of Italian dramatic genius. Gozzi wrote: "I reckon improvised comedy among the particular distinctions of our nation. I look upon it as quite a different species from the written and premeditated drama. The able comedians who sustain the masks are far more praiseworthy than those improvisatory poets who excite astonishment in crowds of gaping listeners." Yet panegyrist Gozzi thus ululates against the "able comedians" of the improvised comedy:

Among all the people to be studied by a philosophical observer none are so difficult to really know as actors and actresses. Educated in deception from the cradle they are such adepts in masking falsehood with an air of candour that it is most difficult to know their true heart and character. The chief idol of all actors is their venal interest. Expressions of politeness, acknowledgments of obligation, terms of praise, courteous welcome are parts of a fixed system of deception which actors consider necessary in the worship of this idol. Barefaced boldness is the chief stock in trade, the very bone and marrow of these artists. There is no sort of impropriety, pretence, injustice, swindling, tyranny which they do not gladly employ.

Let no man suppose that it is possible to converse with actresses without making love. You must make it or pretend to make it. This is the only way to guide them to their own advantage. Love moulds and kneads them in flesh, bones and marrow. Love is their guiding star from the age of five or six. In this respect, I soon discovered that the austerity of Sacchi's company was a barren formula. How many actresses lay siege deliberately and in cold blood to their lovers, despoil them of their property and suck them dry! They worship wickedness and abhor good living. Though they cloak their baseness with the veil of verbal decency, and preserve external decorum, in their souls they trample on shame and sing this verse:

> "Colla vergogna io gia mi sono avvezza."
> (With infamy I long have been at home.)

In what concerned myself I looked upon their love-intrigues as duels of wit and comic passages which furnished me amusement. They would have done anything to gain my heart. Meanwhile, their attentions, protests, fits of rage, jealousies and tears on my account had all the scenic illusion of an overwhelming passion. Self-love is so ingrained in human frailty that men always fancy themselves preferred by the woman on whose very faults they put an indulgent interpretation. This was my case with the Ricci.

Gozzi's pride restrains his giving a true revelation of his love for Teodora Ricci. It was probably the only real romance in his long, lonely and arid life. In a play by Renato Simoni, Gozzi is shown already tormented by his sour temper, jealous disposition and falling a facile prey to the intrigues of Sacchi and of his pupil Teodora Ricci. Ricci is a typical Venetian actress, puerile and fickle rather than wicked, who manages to love Sacchi, Gozzi and Gratarol at the same time. In the last act of Simoni's play Gozzi is a lonely old man. His elderly housekeeper and old-fashioned servants make a comfortless home for the man who has outlived his fame. Sacchi comes in to say good-bye and their meeting is pathetic. Gozzi sits surrounded by his servants and Sacchi, straightening his stooping form, commences one of his traditional scenes. His jokes fall flat, his *lazzi* stir not even a smile. When the worn-out actor throws down his cap, his sobs of despair are echoed by his aged and forlorn patron. They fall into each other's arms, and Gozzi's parting word is a name which now trembles on his lips: "Teodora?"

MARCO AND HIS MARIONETTES ON THEIR TRAVELS

MARIONETTES

Chapter I

Origin of the Italian Marionettes

BEFORE history began there were marionettes; and so long as there are children and grown-ups with the hearts of children still there will be marionettes. A complete history of marionettes would require a vast volume; for their production has been wider and is more ancient than civilization. The Oriental marionettes, the Javanese "Shadows" and "Rounded marionettes," half mythical and religious, half heroic and national, depicting gods, princes and giants; the Siamese "Nang," moving transparent pictures on illuminated screens; the elaborate popular performances of Burmese temple puppets; the high art of the Chinese "Shadow Play," perhaps without equal in its vast range of subjects; the Japanese puppets; the Indian marionette plays, in one of which the god Siva falls in love with a puppet of Parvati, his wife; and the modern marionettes, so popular in the United States; all these specialized subjects have been amply considered by other writers.

Our own inquiry begins with Herodotus who, writing in the fifth century B.C., says that the origin of mechanical dolls dates from remotest antiquity. He saw Egyptian women carrying statuettes in religious processions; the head and body being moved by strings. The monstrous figures of Egyptian gods were marionettes which the priests moved by hidden mechanism. In the Vatican cemetery in 1544 there were found

99

many marionettes which had been buried for more than a thousand years; and in the tombs of Thebes and Memphis in Egypt there have been found ivory and wood painted figures of beasts and men which could be moved by pulling strings, and were probably marionettes, and within the last few weeks (1935) several small lifelike ivory mechanical figures estimated to be two thousand years old have been discovered in an Egyptian tomb.

From the Egyptians the Greeks borrowed marionettes for their religious ceremonies and also for use in the Theatre; some of the manipulators called *Neurospastomena* were celebrated. Many Greek and Roman writers mention them. At Callia's famous banquet, as described by Xenophon, marionettes performed for his guests. To illustrate his discourses Socrates drew lessons from these puppets. The marionette theatre of Antiochus of Cyzicus was furnished with complicated mechanism, the King himself operating large carved figures painted from life. The Athenian Archons allowed a famous *Neurospasta* to erect his puppet-stall in the great theatre of Bacchus, that had witnessed the plays of Euripides; and he spoke through the same masks that had been used by the great tragedians.

Holding up a marionette Plato says: "Friends, let us consider ourselves as living figures sent out from the workshop of the gods . . . our passions are wires or strings pulling us by opposite movements to contradictory actions. Good sense suggests that we should obey one only of these wires resisting all the others. That one wire is the golden wire of reason and law. That one alone is suitable for all movements, because it is of gold, and is stable in form. All the other strings must be subject to that one thread of law . . . because reason would be weak did not law reinforce the composition of the gold wire destined to govern all the others."

In Rome during the religious ceremonies preceding games in the circus wooden statues were carried which moved their heads and pretended to attack one another. As *Rogantino* makes modern Italian children tremble, so in Juvenal's time the little Romans trembled at sight of the *Lamioe* (African ghouls) and *Manducus* "the child eater," a sharp-toothed monster with human head, prototype of the French *Machecroute* and the *Croque-mitaine* who, said Rabelais in *Pantagruel*, "opened large and horrible jaws well lined with teeth top and bottom which, with the help of a small hidden cord, were made to clack terribly against each other." From the Roman religious marionettes were derived the marionettes of the Roman secular theatre, the players being called *neurospastes*. The actors of the *Atellanae* borrowed the *Manducus* from the earlier figure of religious ceremonies. "In this manner was established in Rome an exchange between the living actors of the *Atellanae* and the wooden ones of the marionette theatre." *

Whether living actors or marionettes first appeared on the Greek and Roman stage is uncertain. Probably both acted at the same time and often on the same stage and before the same audience. They dealt with the same social, moral and political problems; praised or ridiculed the same personages. Among the properties of the Roman marionette theatre were fauns with goats' hoofs, hairy satyrs, fat Sileni, enormous priapuses and other personages of the *bacchanalia* and *lupercalia*, marionettes that spoke dialogues (*diverbia*) suggested by the licentious performances and other marionettes as perfect and as wanton as the living dancers they imitated. The mar-

* Charles Magnin.

vellous perfection of the marionettes has been attested by Aristotle in the treatise *De mundo*. The author speaks of the omnipotence of God, who has no need of many means and instruments to move men and all created things "like those mechanics who, by a single device, obtain many varied effects; or like those puppet operators appropriately called *Neurospasti,* who manipulate figures by pulling strings, making the doll move its head and hands, its shoulders and eyes, and sometimes all its members, not without grace and moderation." *

Apuleius, translating the treatise, added the following: "The one directing the movements of the little wooden figures has but to pull the string of the little puppet they wish to put into action and at once the neck bends, the head nods, the eyes move, the hands adapt themselves to all offices and the little figure moves exactly as though living."

In Rome marionettes assumed many forms and were dressed in many ways. There were marionettes for the common people and those for the higher classes; marionettes of the crossroads, porticoes and squares and those of the baths, gymnasia and theatre. Puppets were threaded on a string stretched from knee to knee of the operator who played a musical instrument and moved his legs to the rhythm, the figures wildly throwing their arms and legs in all directions. Other figures danced on the table during banquets. In portable stalls marionettes performed improvised farces; and others performed in their own theatre. So popular were

---

* *"Non secus atque illi Machinatores solent, qui instrumento uno demittendo, multos atque varios effectus edunt; aut ut illi faciunt quos Neurospastas ob id appellant, quod imagunculas animatas esse, fidiculis ductitandis ementiuntur; qui cum funiculum ipsi aut nervum adduxerunt, cieri cervicem et manum, quasi animantis simulacri, humerumque itidem et oculos faciunt interdum etiam omnia membra; atque quadam cum venustate et aequabilitate motus."* Pseud. Aristot.: *De mundo,* cap. vi. Oper. tom. iii. p. 376.

marionettes with the ancient Romans that many writers mention them. In *De se ipso* the Emperor Marcus Aurelius says: "Remember it is your vices that control you as strings control the wooden marionettes. Learn that within you there is something more sublime than puppet-strings . . . death, separating your soul from the tyranny of the senses, will end the wretched state of a marionette in which you are now living."

The repertoire of the Greek and Roman marionette theatre was largely composed of parodies of popular tragedies, and of satiric dialogue aimed at the government and at fashionable vices. The marionettes of Fotino the Greek even parodied the gods. The *Maccus,* a marionette with hunchback and protruding stomach, might be a Pulcinella. The Roman marionettes Pappus, Buccus and Casnar depicting the parasite, glutton, simpleton and rake were transferred to the Atella scenes, creating a popular type of impromptu farce, obscene in word and gesture.

In the early Church Christian priests used marionettes parading monsters and colossal figures; and giant Goliaths and St. Christophers moving their arms and legs were continued during the Middle Ages, in sacred representations, liturgical dramas, mysteries and morality plays. Wild beasts and giants appeared in the episodes of the sacred dramas, serpents hissing and devils rushing round the open door of hell, lions devouring the ministers of the King but sparing Daniel.

St. Clement of Alexandria, Tertullian and Synesius drew moral comparisons and reflexions from the marionette theatres. Medieval churches and monasteries erected wooden stages in the chapels and naves where dramatic episodes of the Passion, the life of the Virgin and of Saints were performed by gorgeously dressed marionettes sometimes covered with jewels and gold. Marionette performances in Italian churches were so prevalent during the early Middle Ages that Innocent III took strong action against their abuse. In course of time these puppet-shows in churches developed into elaborate theatrical performances. When the Council of Trent endeavoured to restrain the abuse of religious marionettes the puppets evaded proscription by passing from the church to the secular theatre.

OTHELLO AND DESDEMONA, MARIONETTES

Chapter II

Italian Marionettes Go Abroad

IT IS said the word "Marionette" may come from *maria, mariola,* diminutives given to small figures of the Virgin, exposed in churches and crossroads. Marote, mariotte and marionette were pet names given to young girls and from this jugglers may have given the name marionette to their wooden dolls. There is another story which relates that in the tenth century at the time of the *Festa delle Marie* ten beautiful Venetian girls gorgeously dressed and wearing rich jewels were walking in procession to the Church of Santa Maria della Salute where they were to be married. Suddenly barbarian pirates rushed in from the sea and dragged the girls to their galleys. The Venetians pursued the infidels, slew the abductors and brought back the brides. From that day, at the *Festa delle Marie* twelve of the most beautiful and most virtuous Venetian girls were superbly dressed at the expense of the Republic and were then married with a dowry from the public treasury. The expense was great, the choice of the girls caused quarrels which were ended by substituting twelve mechanical figures brought forth each year from the storerooms of the Signoria. Of these life-size figures the street venders sold small copies for children to carry about which were called "Marionettes" or little Maries.

In 1550 in Italy, they were called *bagattelli* and *magatelli;* but Burattino, one of the characters in the Italian comedy, became famous in the marionette theatre, gave them his name; and, from the end of the sixteenth century generally, they were called *burattini*. *Burattini* and *fantoccini* are those articulated and moved by wires; *bamboccie,* those which are operated by a horizontal string tied to a stick and to the knee of the one who moves them; *pupi, pupazzi* are those which have head and hands in wood, the body being a cloth pocket in which the thumb and middle finger move the arms and the forefinger moves the head. Spanish marionettes are named *literes* or *bonifrates* because they always represent saints or hermits.

The first efforts of dramatic art in France associated living actors with marionettes in the representation of the Mysteries. At Dieppe in the square in front of the church of St. James, for the festival of the Assumption on August 1st, a company of clergy and laity "supported by marionettes set in motion by means of strings and counterweights" represented the Mystery of the Assumption of the Virgin Mary, in which four hundred *personaggi* took part. At Christmas and Easter and at Corpus Domini festival at Lyons, Paris and Marseilles similar dramatic performances were held. The Birth and Passion of our Lord, the Creation of the World, the Fall of Man, Samson and Delilah, the heroism of Judith, the Prodigal Son, and the Rich Man and Lazarus were represented. In Paris this custom was continued into the seventeenth century. The fathers of the religious order of Theatines constructed a splendid *presepio* in front of their Convent and peopled it with movable wooden figures that greatly delighted the *badauds* and women. Sixteenth century Florentine memoirs mention the use of marionettes and the emigration of Italian puppets to foreign countries in the company of charlatans, surgeons, dentists and venders of quack medicine.

The *Serees* of Guillaume Bouchet, lord of Brocourt, the oldest French book that gives an account of the plays of theatrical burattini (1584), mentions Francatrippa. The Italian Pulcinella, Arlecchino, Pantalone and Colombina are familiar names in French theatres; and in 1649 the first permanent marionette stage was erected in Paris by the side of the Porte de Nesle. The proprietors of that *jeu de marionettes* were Giovanni and Francesco Briocci of Bologna. Francesco carved the little figurines; Giovanni made them speak in French, Italian and Latin to the delight of the Parisians. In a letter addressed to the Princess Mary, daughter of James II of England, Hamilton praises the Pulcinella of Briocci, who was then at the Fair of Saint-Germain in Laye.*

Briocci's ape Fagottino gained celebrity by its tragic death. One day Cyrano de Bergerac saw the ape strolling round the marionette booth and making grimaces. He thought that it was poking fun at his nose "qu'il avait tout défiguré," as Ménage relates, "et à cause duquel il avait tué plus de dix personnes." Angry Cyrano moved towards the ape, whereupon Fagottino drew his tiny wooden sword and put himself on guard. Cyrano rushed at the ape and killed him. This event was celebrated in a pamphlet entitled "Combat de Cyrano de Bergerac contre le singe de Brioche" (Paris, 1655).

Four years afterwards Giovanni Briocci was summoned with his marionettes to the French Court to amuse the

---

* "La le fameux Polichinelle,
   Qui du théâtre est le héros,
   Quoi qu'un peu libre en ses propos,
   Ne fait point rougir la donzelle,
   Qu'il divertit par ses propos."

In his *peau d'arre* Perrault the academician writes:

   "Pour moi j'ose poser en fait,
   Qu'en de certains moments l'esprit le plus parfait,
   Peut aimer, sans rougir, jusqu'aux marionettes."

Dauphin, son of Louis XIV. The account of expenses of the
Royal family in the year 1669, page 44, records as follows:

A Brioche, joueur de marionettes, pour le séjour qu'l a fait à
Saint-Germain-en-Laye, pendant les mois de septembre, octobre et
novembre, pour divertir les Enfants de France, 1365 livres.

After the death of Giovanni, Francesco Briocci took over the
management of the burattini and gained the honour of Bos-
suet's persecution. But the French King defended the Italian
marionettes; and the Minister Colbert enjoined all police
agents to respect and protect Francesco Briocci and his little
wooden figures. The letter is dated 16 October 1676 and appears in the second volume of the *Correspondance Admi-
nistrative sous Louis XIV* published by Depping. Towards the
end of the seventeenth century when both the Brioccis were
dead and had been succeeded by the Frenchman Bertrand,
marionettes began to meddle with politics and religion. Pulcinella on his stage laughed to scorn the hypocrisy of bigots
and the libertinism of reformers, regarding both Catholics
and Protestants as equally wicked and ridiculous. Pantalone
and Arlecchino fought in opposite factions and Pulcinella
effected their reconciliation by means of heavy *legnate,* or
blows.* On 7 February 1686 Achille de Harlay, *procura-*

* In one of the many pamphlets published during the Fronde, 1608–1652, the
Cardinal Mazarin is thus apostrophized:

Adieu, père aux marionettes;
Adieu, l'auteur des Théatins.

And in another entitled *Lettre au Cardinal burlesque:*

Et votre troupe théatine
Ne voyant pas de sûreté
En notre ville et vicomté
A fait Flandre, et dans ses cachettes
A serré les marionettes
Qu'elle faisait voir ci-devant.

tore générale to the parliaments of Paris, wrote the Lieutenant of Police—"To Monsieur de la Reynie, counsellor of the
King in Council"—that the marionettes at the Fair of Saint-
Germain were representing the destruction of the Huguenots,
"serious matter for the Marionettes." Accordingly M. de la
Reynie silenced them temporarily. Then began a long and
bitter struggle with the actors of the "Théâtre français" and
the "Comédie Italienne" and the passion for marionette plays
increased daily.

After the Renaissance puppets acquired great importance,
and in the seventeenth and eighteenth centuries competed
with living actors and singers. In Rome during the Carnival
of 1668 marionettes acted the melodrama *La Comica del cielo*
or *La Baltasara,* by Giulio Rospigliosi, and in 1671 Carlo
Leone asked permission to perform "certain moral puppet
operette" as he had done for many years "in a room in Piazza
Navona without scandal or uproar."

Girolamo Cardano, in his book *De Subtilitate* says:

Were I to enumerate all the wonders the little jointed and
weighted figures of wood are made to do by means of wires, a
whole day would not suffice for it. They fight, hunt, dance, gamble, blow the trumpet and cook.*

Of the puppets threaded through the upper part of the body
with a string he says:

There was no dance, however difficult, that these marionettes
were not able to imitate making the most surprising gestures with
their feet, legs, arms, head and body and striking many extraordinary attitudes. The incomprehensible consists in the singleness
of the string and in its state of continued perfect tension. Often I
have seen puppets put into motion by several strings alternately
tightened and slackened in which there is nothing wonderful.

* Hieron. Cardano: *Mediolanensis medici. Opera.* tom. III. p. 636.

Lorenzo de' Medici, son of Grand Duke Ferdinando I, provided his friends with marionette performances in the elegant theatre of Palazzo Ardinghelli in Parione.

Piero Iacopo Martelli of Bologna (born 1666, died 1727) man of letters and famous statesman, wrote farces for marionettes which he called *Bambocciate,* and of these *Lo Starnuto di Ercole* was perhaps the most perfect sample. Goldoni writes in his *Memorie:*

The author's lively imagination sent Ercole to the land of the Pigmies. These little people, appalled at the sight of an animated mountain with arms and legs, hid themselves in their holes. Plan, development, plot, catastrophes and accidents, all are there; the style is good and well maintained, the thoughts and sentiments all in proportion to the bodies of the personages; the lines too are short, everything announces Pigmies. A gigantic marionette had to be made for the personage of Ercole; but everything made a good effect and it was a very agreeable amusement.

Marionettes also used old Florentine sacred representations, dramas by Cecchi, Chiari, Ildegonda, Roti, Cicognini and many other famous writers, and all Gozzi's fantastic inventions.*

Developing contemporaneously with the real theatre and on parallel lines the marionette theatre reproduced the same characters, variety of dialects and masks as in the *Commedia dell'Arte.* When the latter became extinct the marionettes

---

* In 1681 Francesco Mazzetti, called *Arlecchino,* boasted that his marionette theatre possessed "a great wealth of figures, scenes and very good reciters." In Bologna many puppet shows were given from 1694 to the end of the eighteenth century, both comedies and melodramas. In 1753, performances were suspended by order of the Legate because these lively puppets "were too dissolute in speech." In Venice in 1679 marionettes performed a melodrama by Camillo Badoer; and in 1680 and 1681 by Filippo Acciaioli. Here too in 1746 Antonio Labia, a rich abbot, had "a little wooden theatre" for marionettes "the exact reproduction in miniature of S. Giovanni Grisostomo," the largest theatre in Venice. During the last years of the Venetian Republic there were given numerous puppet shows presenting complete dramas.

perpetuated Pantaloni, Arlecchini, Pulcinelli and Dottori and invented the Roman Cassandrino, an elderly man "nimble, strong, white-haired, well powdered, well groomed" who regularly fell in love with all the pretty women; according to Stendhal, the Romans recognized the caricature of a Monsignor or Cardinal. The Venetian Facanapa is short of stature with big comic face. Insensible to love he takes the world as he finds it and does not try "to straighten dogs' legs" but "preserves his belly for figs as long as possible."

From the year 1697 the Italian comedians in Paris conducted their productions in the French language. They caricatured the Royal favourite Madame de Maintenon in a comedy called *La Fausse Prude*. Their theatre was promptly closed by the police, "His Majesty not finding it convenient to avail himself any longer of their services." Bertrand, who was conducting a puppet theatre at San Lorenzo, immediately declared that he was the legitimate heir of the Italian comedians and installed himself on that stage which had once witnessed the triumphs of Corneille and Racine. But the King ordered the marionettes to quit the Hôtel de Bourgogne and to occupy a small theatre opposite the Rue du Paradis. Thus in France in the eighteenth century began a new life for the little wooden figures, a life of dispute which lasted for fifty years. On the one side were the *burattini* entrenched at the Fairs of Saint-Laurent and Saint-Germain; on the other side were the opera singers, the actors of the Commedia Italiana and of the Théâtre français, each defending his art against all invasions.

Only the three greater theatres had the right to represent musical Opera, tragedies and *commedie nobili*. To the puppets at fairs permission was granted to perform a certain number of farces for two *personaggi* speaking something like the

old *diverbia,* with the additional stipulation that Pulcinella
was always to speak *par le sifflet de la pratique,* that is to say
with the *pivetta* which gives a metallic and shrieking sound.
The law, however, was continually broken. Marionettes in-
vaded the camp of the privileged theatres and plundered its
vast repertory; the quarrel became so bitter that parliament
was called to settle matters. One day Fuzelier would put dumb
personages on the stage acting by mimic art, the next day
Bertrand would revive the custom of *intermezzi* with violin accompaniment. In 1720 a friendly settlement was made
whereby marionettes were licensed to sing, dance and recite
"six or seven at a time."

Then it was that the famous showman Francisque, the poets
Fuzelier, Lesage and Carneval began their work with a *colpo
di maestro* by inventing the *Opéra comique,* that soon became a formidable competitor of the privileged melodrama.
Art had gained a new form of scenic action in the *Opéra comique* invented for marionettes.

A year later, for the puppets of the Fair of San Lorenzo,
Piron wrote an *opera buffa* in three acts; *Le Mariage de
Momus ou la Gigantomachie.* La Place provided *Pierrot Romulus* a parody of the *Romulus* of La Motte, and there were
many others.

The age of gold for burattini had arrived. Favart began
with them his dramatic career, and composed *Polichinelle
comte de Paonfier,* a parody of the *Glorieux* of Destouches. In
1743 the burattini ridiculed Voltaire with parodies of his
Mérope and *Oreste.* The poet's wrath only increased the success of the plays. The glory of the burattini at the two Fairs
lasted until 1790 when the Fairs themselves were suppressed,
and the burattini were dispersed among the towns and vil-
lages. The whole of France was overrun by Italian *bagatelliers*

who brought with them, together with farces and *scenari*, all
the *personaggi* and *maschere* of the smaller Italian theatres.

The eighteenth century was the golden period also for the
Italian fantoccini aided by Carlo Goldoni's dramatic reforms.
The fight between Gozzi and Goldoni, and Goldoni's attempt
to lead the Italian theatre back to ancient traditions, was meat
indeed to the marionette stage. The new comedies were parodied; the authors and actors, caricatured. When Goldoni's
reform had triumphed the marionette theatre inherited the
ancient comedies *a soggetto*. The masks took refuge on the
narrow platform of the puppets, thus returning after centuries to the place of their birth.

Chapter III

The Puppet Theatre and Its Repertoire

IT WOULD be impossible to compile a comprehensive list of all
the plays acted by Italian marionettes. The burattini repertoire during the last three hundred years would rival that of
the best prose theatres. To the old figures and repertoire of
sacred dramas, saintly legends and miracles were added comic
and vulgar elements, episodes borrowed from books of chiv-
alry, legends, ancient Latin comedies as well as impromptu
popular personages and local types. At this time the operators of marionettes improvised most of their dialogue as
the actors of the *Commedia dell'Arte* did later, many of
whom had been marionette operators before becoming actors;
this was the case with Ruzzante, Cherea and Calmo, who by
such humble, modest improvisations became trained in the
play of words and gesticulations *ex abrupto* or *improvvisa-
mente* in which they later became experts.

The space is narrow behind the stage of a puppet theatre;
dark and crowded. Colossal crouching phantoms standing on
a wooden step back of the curtain, leaning against a wooden
beam, with outstretched hands work the puppets while by the
light of a tallow candle they read the part from a copy book
placed on a plank in front of them. The marionette operator
is proud of his theatre, scenes and actors; well understands
the humour of his public and which of the comedies will give
most pleasure. Fifty or sixty puppets hang from greasy walls

114

OTHELLO AND BRABANTIO, MARIONETTES

with expressions of terror; some have contorted arms and twisted legs; the caved-in bodies of others show internal displacements; all have died in spasmodic convulsions.

An ordinary marionette is composed of a head, forearms, hands, legs and body, all carved from wood and about two feet tall. A wire loop joins the neck and body. The arms from elbow to shoulder and the legs from knee to hip are of cloth. A ring in the head receives the crook of an iron rod from which the puppet hangs when not in use. Two threads are attached to the wrists and two other threads to the ankles or knees. Some marionettes move their eyes, mouths and fingers. Tartaglia twists his lips; Rogantino shows his teeth; Stenterello scratches his nose with his finger; Carciofo eats and drinks and moves his fingers as if playing a violin. A marionette company may comprise a hundred puppets. The wooden actresses are respectable. The prima donna's joints are intact, her head steady. The young girl lover is overworked but still is chaste. The serving maid never allows familiarity off stage. The men are bachelors, true Bayards, chevaliers without fear and without reproach.

Tonight the burattini are to play: *La Grandiosa opera intitolata il Belisario, ossia le avventure di Oreste, Ersilia, Falsierone Selinguerro ed il terribil Gobbo.* To this audience the actors are not fantoccini, but heroes. The *grandiosa opera* of Belisario is *sempre battaglie.* Two puppets dressed in armour speak loudly and flourish gigantic swords while Fantoccino goes into convulsions with every movement; his sword thrashing the air dislocates the opposing warrior's anatomy. When he ceases speaking his arms collapse, his head drops drunkenly, his eyes glaze, his sword points to the ceiling, his legs hang in the air as he awaits the answer of his opponent. Save by way of emphasis the feet of these warriors never touch the floor. Ferocious Selinguerra shouts *"Chi sei tu che osi!"*. With a wild spasm of sword and dangling of arms his opponent roars *"Trema! che son il figlio del terribil Gobbo"* and then collapses into silence. *"Ah, ah!"* the other shouts. *"Male hai fatto a palesarlo—non passo piu contenere il mio immenso furor. Preparati a morir!"* And with a galvanic twitch, his heels striking the floor, he defies the bold youth. But the son of the terrible Gobbo rouses from his collapse, waves a challenge.

Now ensues a terrible battle. Salinguerra and his lieutenant attack the son of Gobbo. In their excitement all three rise from the floor; swords clash furiously, legs beat the air while a drum behind the scenes rolls rapidly. Despite terrible blows the son of Gobbo holds his own, his expression unchanged, a supernatural glare in his unwinking eyes. Finally he is struck down still shaking the "fragments of his blade." *"Preparati a morir!"* thunders Selinguerra; all is over with him. Suddenly, clad in complete steel, the *terribil* Gobbo rushes on the stage; striking the floor, waving his sword, he annihilates Selinguerra and his lieutenant. Then the whole army attack Gobbo. Madly they swing the length of the stage, smashing and cutting each other. They fall before the terrible Gobbo, who shaking with spasms hovers above the heaps of slain.

The *Fantoccini* ballet is extraordinary. After the wooden-headed court have seated themselves on the stage and the *corps de ballet* has advanced and retreated, with a tremendous leap the *prima ballerina* appears, knocks her wooden knees together, jerks her head about, salutes the audience with a smile, bounds forward and pausing on her pointed toe turns endless pirouettes in the air; then throwing her wooden hands forward she stops to receive your applause. She surpasses her mortal sister as the ideal surpasses the real. The *fantoccina* is troubled by no jealousies, pricked by no vain ambition, haunted by no remorse; without envy, sorrow, hunger or fear of old age, her youth is perennial and her smile perpetual. How much better a wooden *fantoccina* than a living *ballerina!*

Most popular of marionettes, Arlecchino was born among the valleys of Bergamo. He speaks Venetian because his hearers would not understand the Bergamo jargon. With his dress of red, blue, violet and yellow cloth cut in triangles and pieced together from top to bottom, a little cap covering his shaven head, he wears slippers without soles and a black mask with tiny holes to see through. That black mask is the ancient face covered with soot. The hiding of his hair beneath his cap is the shaven head obligatory to the *Planipedes.*

Arlecchino is a mixture of ignorance, ingenuity, wit, stupidity and grace. A rough sketch of a man, a grown-up baby; in all of whose stupidities there is mingled cunning. He is a patient, faithful, credulous servant; always in love, always embarrassed about himself, and about his master; as easily afflicted and consoled as a child, his sorrow is as exhilarating as his joy.*

Listen to Arlecchino seeking service:

Sior Florindo, I know you are in need of a serving man. I do everything; eat, drink, sleep, love the maids and dislike work. I will be more faithful than a thief, as secret as an earthquake, and as attentive as a cat.†

Infamous Brighella also hails from Bergamo. Bold with women, cringing with men, overbearing with the weak, cowardly with the strong, relentless when in fear, he handles the knife treacherously; but he has some virtues. Hear his own account of his life:

* Marmontel.
† For further description of Arlecchino see Chapter V of Masks, pp. 72 et seq.

Oh, I make no bones about it! . . . at twelve years old I went to prison, at fifteen in the pillory, at twenty to the whipping post, at twenty-five to the galleys. Grammar, the humanities, rhetoric and philosophy; I have put zeal into all my studies. It is thus I have served my Prince on land and sea. Now I am a hunter and live by what I kill; but none may call me a thief—a clever mathematician rather, who finds things before the owners have lost them. Dear Sior Florindo, by engaging me you will surely win even the most desperate cases. In intrigue I surpass all women; in humbugging, the world's greatest impostors; in evasion, all the gypsies of Egypt; in wrangling, all the lawyers; in business, all the charlatans; in finding expedients, all the musical opera impresarios, and for lies, all of Europe's gazetteers.*

Today, Brighella is more prudent. He rarely assassinates, he steals less, deceives women in love rather than men in business. He strings tender words together. To the charming Smeraldina he declares: "Siora, inspecting my interior I find that your pickpocket eyes have stolen my heart. Restore to me this precious entrail I beg you, generously adding a portion of your own heart, in order that I may avoid suing you in Cupid's court." Brighella also is a serving man, and wears a dark half-mask and black moustaches. He dresses in doublet, pantaloons and a white cloak with green frogs.

The third marionette mask, the *Dottore,* is from Bologna. He dresses in black with chocolate-coloured half-mask and has red cheeks. He knows everything by halves from hearsay and pours forth ridiculous nonsense on every subject. He pretends to be an Academician of the Crusca, a doctor, notary, lawyer or astrologer.

Rogantino is a direct descendant of that Pyrgo-polinices to whom Plautus has given immortality with the nickname of *Miles Gloriosus.* He is a braggart, threatening to eat his enemies alive. He draws his sword only to be ignominiously

* *Generici Birghelleschi.* Novara. Grotti. 1870.

cudgelled. He walks by leaps and bounds and turns his head
to see who dares to open his mouth while he is near. Rogantino was born in Rome in the Pope's army, but he leaps
through the centuries to hang his wire on the hook of ancient
tradition. His body is dwarfed, but he swears, beats his heels
upon the pavement. When he shakes himself he makes his
cartridge-box, bayonet, sword and spurs rattle.

Carciofo is a Neapolitan puppet; big of head, lean of body;
ruddy, reckless and stupid. Born at Pisa in the Belle Torri
theatre, his father was the eldest son of a marionette operator
famed throughout Tuscany and Romagna. One evening as
the performance was about to begin, this Tertulliano stood at
the door urging people to enter when an artilleryman el-
bowed his way forward dragging his reluctant companion.
The embarrassed recruit came zigzagging along, lamenting
the few pence of expenditure. Tertulliano looked at the recruit and Carciofo was born. Carciofo is an astonishing personage. His body sways as he walks with bent knees, his head,
mouth, eyes and shoulders, moving. He drinks, smokes, eats
macaroni, takes the candle from the table to light his pipe.

A very ancient marionette is the Diavolo with all the attri-
butes and characteristics of his infernal nature. At the end of
the eighteenth century the Devil-marionette was so popular
that he married and peopled the stage with numerous offspring, Mago, Fata, Genio and Mostro, indispensable personages in the marionette repertoire. On the stage of the wooden
dolls the diabolic offspring still is honoured, but papa *Diavolo*
though living now plays a very secondary rôle. His shrunken
head is bald and roughly tinted with red and black; his bat's
wings are worn, his horns nibbled, his tail rat-eaten. The
other masks of the puppet theatre, Stenterello, Meneghino,

Gianduja, Gerolamo and Tartaglia, are the same as the living actors of the big theatres.

Always Pulcinella has been the life and soul of the marionette theatre. He was called Pullicinella in Rome and Naples, Pulcinella in the rest of Italy, Polichinelle in France, Punch in England, Hans-Wurst in Germany and Don Christóval Pulichinelo in Spain. His figure is represented in the bronze statuette of Museo Capponi, dressed in a wide sack of white with a narrow leather belt at the waist, a soft conical hat on his head; his face covered with a black half-mask, his nose is hooked and there is a large mole on his cheek. This head and sack form the perfect type of primitive marionette, easily worked with three fingers by an able operator. Today Pulcinella is in service, sharp or stupid according to circumstances, temperate or jealous, talkative or taciturn, lively, sarcastic, always quarrelsome. Pulcinella in Naples, Gerolamo in Milan, Gianduja in Turin, Stenterello in Florence, Brighella and Arlecchino in Venice and the Dottore in Bologna, as marionettes, have kept alive the memory of the *Commedia dell'Arte*.

The wooden dolls of the Fiando theatre in Milan were extremely popular during the early nineteenth century. A French newspaper wrote:

The head, arms and body of these little figures move with so much grace and in such perfect accord with the sentiment expressed by the voice, that except for proportions one could well have imagined he was witnessing a performance of actors of the *Comédie Française*. The classic tragedy *Nabuccodonosor* was given that evening and an Anacreontic ballet entitled *La Delizie di Flora*. The dancers and sylphids of the Paris Opera, so proud of their fine legs and smiling faces, might well envy these charming wooden people who easily overcome the most terrific difficulties of choreographic art.

In his book *De Paris à Naples* M. Jal speaks in the same way of the Milanese puppets.

In his *Roba di Roma* William Story tells us of the Roman burattini he saw in Piazza Navona:

The love for the acting of puppets is universal among the lower classes throughout Italy and in some cities, especially in Genoa, no pains are spared in their costume, construction and movement to render them life-like. . . . The audience listen with grave and profound interest. Every evening there are two performances. We arrived at the Teatro Emiliano just too late for the first. "What is that great noise of drums inside?" we asked. *"Battaglie,"* said the ticket-seller. "Shall we see a battle in the next piece?" *"Eh, sempre battaglia"*—always battle—was the reproving answer.

In Rome the marionette theatre was established in Palazzo Fiano and obtained the privilege of remaining open the whole year.

Henri Beyle, better known as Stendhal, described these Roman puppets:

It was nine o'clock in the evening when I entered Palazzo Fiano. At the door an individual was shrieking: "This way, this way, gentlemen. The performance is about to begin." I paid my half a *paolo* and entered fearful of fleas and bad company, but I was soon reassured. My neighbours were the fattest bourgeois of Rome. And no people better understand and appreciate subtle satire. Laughter has fled to the marionettes who by improvisation flout censorship. The fashionable marionette Cassandrino is a sprightly man of fifty or sixty; as active, upright, powdered, clean and alert as a Cardinal. Expert in business, able conversationalist, Cassandrino would be all virtue did he not fall madly in love with all the women. Cassandrino is of all times and Rome is full of Messeigneurs like him.

The comedy performed that evening was *Cassandrino allievo d'un pittore*. A Roman artist has a sister, beautiful, young and honourable. Cassandrino enters the house under pretence of protecting the artist; he falls in love with the beautiful girl. On account of his age and position he does not dare to make an open declaration of his love. He talks about music and sings a *cavatina* he has heard in a concert. The *cavatina* by Paesiello was exquisitely sung behind the scenes by a girl of the "company," a cobbler's daughter. But while the old man is warbling the artist arrives and reproves his sister and turns Cassandrino out for making love to a girl without being able to marry her.

In the following act the lover reappears disguised as a student with dyed hair and false moustache. He offers the girl much money and a house in the country where they can pass happy days together. Cassandrino is caught by the artist's aunt, a crazy old maid who once was intimate with him and who claims that he must now marry her. After many absurd adventures Cassandrino takes the old maid as his housekeeper and thus becomes in a way the girl's "protector."

Stendhal also describes the Florentine marionettes he saw at the house of a rich merchant. Upon a stage barely five feet wide twenty-four beautifully made puppets eight inches high acted Machiavelli's *Mandragora*. He also mentions Neapolitan marionettes who performed political satires in a private theatre. Of these plays the most applauded was called *Si farà o no un Segretario di Stato?*

In Genoa no pains are spared to render the burattini lifelike. They are made of wood, generally from two to three feet tall with large heads, glaring eyes, and clad in tinsel, velvet and steel. Though the largest are only about half the height of a man, the stage and all the appointments and scenery are in the same proportion and the eye soon accepts them as life size. But if a hand or arm of one of the wire pullers appears its size is startling. The plays are mostly heroic, romantic and historical, startling in incident, imposing in style and grandiose in movement; wars of the Paladins, adventures of knights and ladies, tragedies of the Middle Ages, prodigies of the melodramatic world. Doughty warriors continue to battle until the stage is covered with corpses; they rescue injured damsels, express themselves in boastful language and are equally admirable in love and war.

It has been estimated that there are about forty thousand theatrical puppets in Italy. In the southern provinces of the peninsula puppets are highly esteemed. Large towns hardly know other dramatic performances than those of the marionettes. In Naples, Gaeta, Salerno, Aquila and Caserta, mechanical theatres compete with the larger stages. Marionettes wander all over Italy. The comedies, drama, pantomimes and grand ballets presented by Nocchi in his little Leghorn theatre once competed with celebrated theatrical performances.

Before the World War, in Milan and the Lombardy provinces there were many companies of fantoccini. Those of the Prandi brothers of Brescia made the round of Tuscany, meeting with applause at Florence, Sienna and Pisa. The ballets became regular choreographic performances with elaborate scenic effects and good orchestral music. Placards announced the names of the scene-painter, producer, theatrical costumer and orchestral conductor, with "thirty professors who will not long remain anonymous."

To the ballet dancers have been added gymnasts, acrobats and jugglers; burattini who do rope dancing and trapeze swinging without visible thread to support them; puppets who juggle with balls, bottles and swords, who let off guns, fence, leap through hoops, play the violin with full orchestral

accompaniment. It is no longer the simple ingenuous marionette play of former times.

The burattini theatre has shown the contemporary tend-
encies of philosophy and criticism. Great men and popular
personages, the heroes of religion and of atheism, Beelzebub,
Victor Emmanuel and Garibaldi, Rinaldo di Montalbano,
Joan of Arc, the Nun of Cracow—all of them have found
among the marionettes an hour of resurrection. The present-
day repertoire is still more eclectic. The use of dances has en-
larged the field of marionette scenes.

Hear how Giovan Battiste Fagiuoli speaks to Consiglier
Magalotti of the fêtes given by Cardinal de' Medici in his
Lappeggi villa:

But that which outweighed all other pleasures
And where the money was spent well by all, amusing ears and eyes,
Was the turret of the marionettes.
Oh, what a joy, how fine a thing, to see those puppets fight.
Above all the rest, that Pulcinella.
Has ever man been seen more pleasing in dress, in action, and in
    speech?
And he, poor thing, how unfortunate is he,
Subjected to oppression every minute, or else belaboured all the
    time,
And yet with courage ne'ertheless,
"Victory," he cries, and rings his bell, passing it off in fun.
For no embarrassments for great minds
Have misfortunes, and under the blows of destiny moustaches
    must be kept upturned.

The public of the wooden dolls has changed. The marionette was the most ancient actor, so the marionette theatre is
the most modern. Just as the puppets were transformed when
ancient society became modern society and pagans became
Christians, and from being ecclesiastical and ritual they be-

came laymen and artistic; just as Macco and Centunculo first became the Almighty and the prophet Daniel and Pulcinella and Arlecchino, so now they tend to become political ministers and deputies. In all ages the marionettes have closely followed the transformations of the theatre and of society.

INDEX

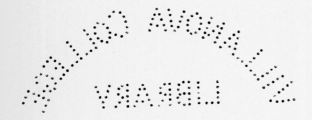